MW00563663

BODY PHOBIA

DIANNA E. ANDERSON

BODY
PHOBIA

THE WESTERN
ROOTS of our FEAR
of DIFFERENCE

Broadleaf Books
Minneapolis

BODY PHOBIA
The Western Roots of Our Fear of Difference

Copyright © 2024 Dianna E. Anderson. Published by Broadleaf Books, an imprint
of 1517 Media. All rights reserved. Except for brief quotations in critical articles or
reviews, no part of this book may be reproduced in any manner without prior written
permission from the publisher. Email copyright@1517.media or write to Permissions,
Broadleaf Books, PO Box 1209, Minneapolis, MN 55440-1209.

"Body Was Made"
Words and Music by Ezra Mordechai Furman
Copyright © 2015 Ice Chest Musick
All Rights Administered Worldwide by Kobalt Songs Music Publishing
All Rights Reserved Used by Permission
Reprinted by Permission of Hal Leonard LLC

Library of Congress Cataloging-in-Publication Data

Names: Anderson, Dianna E., author.
Title: Body phobia : the western roots of our fear of difference / Dianna
    E. Anderson.
Description: Minneapolis : Broadleaf Books, [2024] | Includes
    bibliographical references.
Identifiers: LCCN 2023046489 (print) | LCCN 2023046490 (ebook) | ISBN
    9781506496436 (hardback) | ISBN 9781506496443 (ebook)
Subjects: LCSH: Human body--Social aspects--United States. | Difference
    (Psychology) | Other (Philosophy)--United States. | Fear--United States.
Classification: LCC HM636 .A63 2024 (print) | LCC HM636 (ebook) | DDC
    302--dc23/eng/20231019
LC record available at https://lccn.loc.gov/2023046489
LC ebook record available at https://lccn.loc.gov/2023046490

Cover image: © 2023 Shutterstock; Female dummy with broken arms
and legs/559819384 by Bernd Rehorst
Cover design: Michelle Lenger

Print ISBN: 978-1-5064-9643-6
eBook ISBN: 978-1-5064-9644-3

Printed in India.

To Marc and Carrie, without whom my life
would be far less fun.

CONTENTS

INTRODUCTION

Math class had a strange effect on me when I was in high school. It was the last period of the day, and at least once a month, I would have to leave to go to the nurse's office. Something would happen where my brain would offer, unprompted: "How awful would it be if you puked right now?" And I couldn't stop. I would start feeling nauseated and work myself up into a fervor. One time, the spiral of thoughts got so loud that my teacher took one look at me and sent me into the hall with a trash can to go to the nurse.

I got five feet from the door and slammed the plastic bin onto the floor, leaning over it like a 35-year-old realizing they aren't 21 anymore. I looked up to see two upperclassmen staring at me with looks of alternating disgust and concern. I hadn't actually thrown up, but I was making noises like I was going to. Even more embarrassed now, I picked up the trash can and ran to the nearby bathroom, throwing myself into a stall, kneeling on the floor until I caught my breath. This would repeat several times throughout the year, playing out in varying levels of dramatic fashion. Sometimes I just needed to go to the bathroom to breathe. Other times it was a full phone call home and a request for me to be picked up early. I went to the doctor to see what was going on, and the doc—now the head of the hospital twenty years later—shrugged his shoulders and said, "Maybe it's a stomach bug. Or your period."

It was neither of those things. It was, in fact, an anxiety disorder. It's been with me since I was a kid—I look back on my childhood now, and I recognize the ways in which my seemingly strange moods and sudden meltdowns in public were actually the result of complete and total fear overtaking my body. My mom wondered if I was doing something to avoid math class in particular, but it turned out that it just happened to be my last class of the day. By the time I got there, all my defenses that had kept anxiety at bay for most of the day were wearing out and failing.

As an evangelical Christian at the time, I spent years praying to be well, to have whatever was wrong with me taken away. I lived constantly in fear of my own body and what it may do in the future. It helped me somewhat to picture my body as a thing outside of myself, an object that I was battling. And after all, this way of thinking about my body comported very well with the culture in which I was raised— bodies are objects to be feared and controlled by this thing called the soul, or the real self.

What I didn't realize was that fear was driving so many of my life decisions. I missed out on opportunities, lost jobs, broke up friend-ships, and ended up miserable by the age of twenty-seven because I could not figure out how to handle this fear. Instead of battling it, I was embracing it, disconnecting myself from my body as an enemy at war. I was afraid—afraid of appearing to be different, of having a body that had visible needs in public, of being *seen* as a frail, mortal human. Being seen as having a body at all cranked up my anxiety to eleven, emphasizing the fear of being perceived as different that dictated much of my early life. I wanted desperately to be *normal* and fearing my own body was the way through.

And I realized: I'm not alone. As I used my own fear as justification for my behavior—my anxiety made me feel the need to justify myself and keep digging in arguments I wasn't qualified to be involved in—I also saw how fear was the common logic, the common string that ran through cultural controversies, political movements, and discussions about where society is "going." Fear is the justification for an officer's knee on a Black man's neck. Fear is the reason disabled people were kept in institutions. Fear of a "contagious" transgender identity shuts down clinics and denies young people access to necessary health care.

When I look back on it, it's entirely unsurprising that American culture is characterized by fear, especially in my generation. The World Trade Center towers fell when I was fifteen, and I remember the immense anxiety and anger that gripped the American public. The fear we felt from that act of terrorism was the justification for invading two countries on the other side of the world. But before then, there was the school shooting in Columbine and Timothy McVeigh in Oklahoma City. We are deeply afraid of what other people's actions can do to our culture and "way of life."

Looking back, it also becomes clear how much of this fear relied on pretending we did not have bodies or that the bodies we did have were things to fear. Fear led white Americans to create a phenomenology (a philosophy of experience) of the body that deprioritizes the physical experience, prioritizes the mind alone, and imposes on society an idea of a person as a vague, amorphous soul, not a body restricted by physics and space and with limitations.

Once I noticed, I began seeing this phenomenology everywhere in American culture, from how evangelicals talk about life after death, to wellness culture convincing people that the best way to live is to disappear your own body into thinness, to how people with non-normative bodies were treated in the "culture wars," be they fat, trans, disabled, or of color. There was also, I noticed, an underlying question of who gets to move beyond their body and who is confined to it and forced to reckon with it at all times. Whiteness and abled-ness and cisgender normativity dictate so much about how American culture approaches and lands upon The Body, depending on whose body is being examined. Fear of bodies that are *different* are at the root.

British YouTuber and actress Abigail Thorn, who posts videos under the name Philosophy Tube, spoke in her video (where she came out as trans) about the "mind in a jar" problem. French philosopher René Descartes famously asked how he could know whether he truly existed—whether his body was indeed real or just a projection of his mind. He went on to argue that while he could not be sure that even his own body exists, he can be sure that this thing called "I" that had thought—cognition—was real, and therefore he as a human was likely real. *Cogito ergo sum*—I think, therefore I am.

But Thorn points out that such thought is only possible if you exist in a world where your humanity is a given, where you are not constantly at odds with other people who treat you as a nothing, as a thing that looks human but has no internal life making it human. Thorn sums it up like this:

> The philosopher Charles Mills has pointed out that you have to be pretty secure in your life to question whether the world and other people exist. He says that if you were, for example, a black person in the United States like Audre Lorde was, the question "do other people exist" might seem kind of frivolous because you are very used to the idea that other people control large parts of your life. It seems weird to doubt that the world is there because you feel the mental friction that occurs when you move through it. Descartes had to convince himself that other people were real, but Audre Lorde had to convince other people that she was.[1]

All of us live and exist in a culture where only some of us get to be considered human, as having an inner life worth protecting and understanding. The dominant idea in American culture is instead fear—fear of the Other, fear of the reality of the body, fear of what it means to exist in physical space. For this, we take our lessons from those who have come before because, as Audre Lorde herself says, "If history has taught us anything, it is that action for change directed only against the external conditions of oppression is not enough. In order to be whole, we must recognize the despair oppression plants within each of us—that thin persistent voice that says our efforts are useless, it will never change, so why bother, accept it."[2]

That's the project before you here: to examine the American fear of the body, how it permeates all parts of culture, and who gets to be perceived as more than their body and who does not. My own fear of my body guides this project as I explore what science says about the body and the mind, what traditions outside of WASP (White, Anglo-Saxon Protestant) Christianity say, and how different instances of marginalization impact the body in different ways. It's time to delve deep into why we are such anxious, depressed messes and understand that the root cause is probably our brains but also our complete disconnect from our flesh, our bodies, our mortality.

And in the course of that examination, we'll uncover the reality of the fear behind the various prejudices we characterize as phobias—homophobia, transphobia, fatphobia. At the root of our prejudices is the refusal and fear of recognizing the shared humanity of the shared bodily experience and how those experiences shape who we are.

In pursuit of change, of recognizing who gets to be embodied and who is forcibly disembodied, we will pull from those who have come before, those whose work sits at the intersections of Black, gay, trans, disabled, and Othered. Like Lorde, we will seek to render visible and excise that poison of Othering of our bodies that dominant oppressions have rendered so meaningless, a reclamation of the inner life as well as a fight for the outer.

Confronting this demon won't be easy. It means tearing open old wounds, scars long healed over pulled open and stitched up again. It means being willing to become Frankenstein's monster for a time, even if only to see how we have stitched our ideas of the self together from Gnostic tales and a dualism thought up by men who never had their right to exist challenged in any meaningful way. And it means, if you're willing, liberation.

1 | THE RELIGIOUS BODY

I used to live in the suburbs of Chicago, in what feels like another lifetime. I worked for the Christian Reformed Church of America, which, if you know me now, sounds like an absolutely hilarious place for me to end up. And it was—it's no surprise that I didn't last long in that role, getting fired from it because I was no longer a "culture fit," and stopped attending weekly chapel with my coworkers because it gave me anxiety. But during the two years I lived in the Chicago area, I took advantage of my first time in a large metro area by experiencing all it had to offer, including visiting the Billy Graham Center at Wheaton College. Now, to be clear, my intention in visiting there wasn't exactly pure—I'd heard about how goofy the center's exhibits were and wanted to see it for myself. Foremost on my list was the Heaven Room.

The Heaven Room at the Billy Graham Center is the culmination of a self-guided tour that is meant to be an evangelism technique. After touring the museum and learning about Graham's life and legacy, there's a section where you are walked through the gospel message and led toward the cross and invited to take part in salvation. As part of this messaging, you are guided into a room that is a simulation of "heaven." Painted clouds on the walls, with a mirrored ceiling and floor designed to make it look like the clouds go on infinitely, the Heaven Room echoes with praise music from a recorded choir.

1

It is, in a word, cheesy. And it's somehow meant to inspire the viewer into conversion (I have to wonder if it has any kind of success rate). It proposes a version of the afterlife, of both this life and whatever comes after we die that is . . . boring. Souls up in the clouds, singing worship songs in a choir for eternity, our individualism erased, nothing but an ongoing worship service for the rest of time.

But this is the vision of one of the most powerful political and religious movements of our time—that this life we have here is temporary, that our flesh simply does not matter, and that we will eventually be lifted into the air to meet with God. Billy Graham was an immensely important evangelist, leading a revival of Christianity across America and leaving a long legacy that includes his son, Franklin Graham, becoming something of a kingmaker in American conservative politics, throwing his considerable power behind the Trump administration.

Growing up, I was immersed heavily in this culture, listening to music and reading books that celebrated the time we'd be in heaven, that everything about this world would melt away and we'd be in this strange liminal space where we exist as souls. This comported well with my own disconnect from my body—if our bodies were merely vessels, then I didn't need to care about decorating mine or what it looked like at the end of the day. I retreated into a life of the mind, convinced that I could leave my own body behind and merely act as a vessel for God's work.

But by the time I visited the Heaven Room at the Billy Graham Center in Wheaton, I'd given up, largely, on that way of thinking. There was something wrong with the way in which my synapses fired in my brain that made functioning in my body nearly impossible. My life had been overtaken by an anxiety disorder. Sometimes I was unable to leave the house even to get groceries, making it impossible for me to attend events I so dearly wanted to attend (I could've met Rachel Maddow if my brain and body had cooperated!). I had learned that my body *mattered* and had mattered all along—there was no "me" without this body that rebelled and made daily life so hard. I could not simply will myself into a different form.

I should've known this, considering I'd been obsessed with the idea of what it meant to be "fully human" in college. A theology nerd, I was deeply concerned with what it meant for Jesus to come to earth as flesh and bone, to be born and to live as human. These thoughts guided my academic pursuits throughout college. When it came time to write our fifteen-page paper for our senior year systematic theology course, I chose to tackle the question of whether or not Jesus was capable of sin—if he was *fully human* and *fully divine*, is the capacity to sin part of that humanity? Was sin carried in the body?

That paper got me voted "mostly likely to become an academic studied by others" by the rest of the theology cohort, but even after ADHD hyper-focusing and writing all fifteen pages on a Saturday afternoon, I still didn't quite have an answer I was satisfied with, perhaps because I didn't yet have the framework to what being human *means*. I had yet to begin my work on the mind–body problem, so entrenched was I in the evangelical theology that proclaimed, in words misattributed to C. S. Lewis: "You are a soul and you have a body." The quote actually appears to have originally been attributed to George MacDonald and appeared more popularly in Canticle for Leibowitz, a 1959 science fiction classic.[1] But the prevalence of it within American Christian culture had led to a further entrenching of a form of dualism (a sharp division between the mind and the body) that had guided my thinking for most of my life. Bodies exist to be vessels for our souls for the moment, for the temporary reality we exist in now, rather than defining features of our lives. After all, I was raised evangelical.

Evangelicals are a religious minority with an outsized impact on the culture. Since the 1960s, white evangelicals have been an important political bloc for the right wing to court—George W. Bush won reelection in large part because he motivated evangelicals to vote based on a desire to stop marriage equality and abortion. In 2016, in spite of the Republican candidate being a thrice-married adulterer who has, in all likelihood, paid for a few abortions in his time, evangelicals overwhelmingly voted for him, with many evangelical celebrities endorsing Trump outright. And evangelicalism in modern days has a theology of the body that rejects most of the body and/or views it as a thing separate from the Self as Human, a thing to be controlled rather than understood.

This way of thinking has, I believe, heavily shaped American politics throughout the last sixty or so years that evangelicalism has been a powerful political bloc and bastion of white politics. That is no error—Dr. Anthea Butler, professor of religion at the University of Pennsylvania, writes that evangelicalism as we know it today emerged as a reaction to the Civil Rights movement of the 1950s and 1960s. It sought out reasoning that would allow it to follow the shifting winds against explicit racism and instead embrace a theology that still was, at its center, white. To do this, they found dualism and the colorblind gospel: "This color-blind gospel is how evangelicals used biblical scripture to affirm that everyone, no matter what race, is equal and that race does not matter. The reality of the term 'color-blind,' however, was more about making Black and other ethnic evangelicals conform to whiteness and accept white leadership as the norm both religiously and socially."[2] Dualism functioned to disregard the body and therefore to disregard the ways racism acted upon the body itself, the individual, and their life. If we are all merely souls, there is no need then to confront or deal with racism because we are all treated the same (like white people). This colorblind gospel was aided by citations of verses like Galatians 3:28, that we are all one in Christ Jesus and there is no Jew nor Gentile.[3]

Butler goes on to write that the 1990s saw attempts to work toward reconciliation between races in evangelicalism, often cynically deployed to court Black voters into voting conservatives into office.

But some of it was genuine, however tainted as it was by a continued dualistic approach to the body. For evangelicals, racism is not a corporate sin—a sin that is system wide and needs examining of theological standards and ideas in order to fully root out—but rather an individuated one of relationship. Because white evangelicals refused to grasp the ways in which *systems* function to perpetuate racism, racism was instead downgraded to an individual racist attitude, always with the conception that it is an individual warping theology in order to sin, rather than theology that might be an issue.

This avoidance of looking at systemic issues reveals a portion of the rot that is the deeply American theology of the body. Because evangelicalism's conception of the body is deeply gnostic, pointing instead to heaven and casting the human body as simply a brief stop on the heavenward journey—D. L. Moody, famous evangelist for whom the Moody Bible Institute in Chicago is named, referred to his body on earth as "an old clay tenement"—issues that confront the body in physical space cannot be approached with any seriousness. To be sure, in many ways evangelicalism is *obsessed* with the body—but only insofar as it is a thing to control, a mechanism by which one can force their souls toward God.

Even attempted corrections to these dualistic tendencies distance the self from the body. Matthew Lee Anderson (no relation) wrote what purported to be a corrective to the evangelical dualism of the body in 2011, *Earthen Vessels*. But as an evangelical, Anderson finds himself unable to escape from language that casts the body as a separate *other*, a thing to be subdued. In one section, he rightly notes that evangelicals are at best inattentive to the body, only noting the possibility for God's work when bodies are seen as broken, such as in faith healing. But as a corrective, he offers that focus on healing is too narrow a focus, "rather than God's power to sanctify the body through reforming its habits and dispositions."[4] Isn't reforming and sanctifying simply another word for *healing*, just in the spiritual sense?

Anderson goes on to frame the body as a thing that develops subconscious affirmations of potentially false reality—in other words, how we *behave* in the world reflects what we really believe about it. The problem, for Anderson, is not that evangelicals have developed a dualism that prioritizes heaven but that evangelicalism has been too inattentive to how the body can be used and subdued to achieve those heavenward aims. While acknowledging and getting close to the idea that the physical body is who we are, Anderson eventually circles back around to the idea that bodies are tools for us to shape and move: "Our bodies are organized by the ends and goals we pursue."[5] While Anderson understands that bodies have limits, he never fully addresses how differently constructed bodies—particularly differently radicalized bodies—shape experiences of the world. Even as he addresses how the body interacts with the world and with society, he chooses instead to focus on abortion, consumerism, and individualism rather than the quite obvious elephant in the room of racism. And on the question of homosexuality—to which he dedicates an entire chapter—he writes that the central problem is "whose body is it?"[6] To whom does this body belong?

Anderson is a fairly typical evangelical, albeit in my experience more thoughtful than most. But his work attempting to correct an ongoing problem within evangelicalism suffers from a flaw that cannot be rooted out without changing the very foundations of modern American evangelicalism: that the body is not important. In all his attempts to reframe the discussion, the body exists as this problem floating in the background, and Anderson's conclusion, eventually, is to subdue the physical through the use of the spiritual. The body should be physically incorporated into spiritual disciplines that enhance the personhood inhabiting the body rather than viewed as the person itself.

This dualistic theology that separates the person and the body is well worth examining. Much of evangelical theology emphasizes (perhaps overemphasizes) the works of the apostle Paul, a zealot and Christian convert who was working in the first century to establish churches across the known world at the time. Converted through direct intervention from God on the road to Damascus, Paul's view of the world has shaped much of Christian theology from the moment his letters to the early churches were canonized as Scripture. Paul frequently positioned "the flesh" and the spirit as separate beings, hinging much of his theology and work on Christ in a Platonic dualism that attempted to integrate flesh and spirit. This dualism has pervaded evangelical and Christian theology to this day. Indeed, as Americans, it's impossible to separate white Americanism from this culturally conservative vision of the body, as our founding as a "Christian nation" is heavily rooted in the deeply conservative Protestantism of our forebears. Even if a person doesn't identify as evangelical, Paul's theology interpolated through the lens of the particular American Protestant view of the body is still impacting their everyday lives.

Indeed, it is Paul's Platonism that works to separate Christianity from the previous radical sects of Judaism from which it emerged. With the emergence of a new Christian sect, new moralities and conceptions about the human body were likewise forming, largely as a response to paganism throughout Rome but also to develop a sense of understanding of themselves as a community and a minority religious practice in a society ruled by rich nobles. Peter Brown, a scholar of late antiquity around this period, writes that a driving force in both Jewish and early Christian communities was to develop a "singleness of heart,"[7] that is, to develop solidarity within the community, to forgo deceptiveness or duplicity or egotism, and instead to give oneself to the survival of the community. Brown points out that this was largely down to how the community interacted with physical space and the stratification of the class structure in which many of the early Christians live. In urban environments, which were dependent on the generosity of a ruling class, "Much of what is claimed as distinctively

'Christian' in the morality of the early churches was in reality the distinctive morality of a different segment of Roman society from those we know from the literature of the wellborn."[8] Early Christians, being composed of lower-class and poor members of the populace, could not develop their sense of themselves as a community apart from their bodily situation, and therefore, they developed a morality that centered on mutual aid and respectable familial relationship.

Here is where Christianity and Judaism diverged: for early Christians, sexual discipline came to "bear the full burden of expressing the difference between themselves and the pagan world."[9] Sexual restraint, monosexual culture, and a restrained sexual ethic came to characterize early Christianity as a rejection of the sexuality of the pagan world. It was, as Brown notes, pretty much the only moral discipline that was available to early Christians, and it became a locus of control for the community as a differentiation from the rest of Roman society. Brown rightly asks, "Why is the body singled out by being presented in consistently sexual terms—as the locus of imagined recesses of sexual motivations and the center of social structures thought of sexually—as being formed originally by a fateful sexual drive to marriage and childbirth?"[10]

Like Adam and Eve eating from the forbidden tree and seeing their nakedness for the first time, this concept of the body as only ever sexual affected how I saw my own body. Around the time I first started wearing "real" bras—the kind with snaps and clasps, not just soft fabric I could pull over my head—I had to have my mom help me put on a strapless bra for my dress for my brother's wedding. I instinctively crossed my arms over my breasts when my shirt came off, afraid of my own nakedness in front of the person who had literally given birth to me. After all, I was brought up in a world where the body's nakedness was linked strongly with the original sin. No wonder Saint Augustine lamented sex as a whirlpool from which there is no escaping. We'll return to the sexuality question later on, but it is important here that early Christian morality centered itself around the conception of *controlling* the body, particularly sexually, and therefore created the perfect conditions for distancing one's self from the body. And it is no coincidence that this shift happened as Christianity was aligning itself with power in the form of the State (Emperor Constantine).

The divorce of Christianity from a religion of the embodied to one in which the body is subsumed to a system of power has been an evolution throughout the centuries of Christian thought, but it received its biggest boost in the Protestant Reformation and its fallout. This is central to the development of the peculiarly American theology of the body, which is the subject of this book. In a reinterpretation particularly of the apostle Paul, figures of the Reformation—Martin Luther and John Calvin, prized in evangelical circles—rebelled against what they saw as unholy practices that placed salvation as a thing that could be bought or sold through works rather than a matter of faith alone. The apostle Paul takes an apocalyptic view of the world, as he believed Christ's return was imminent and thus the physical world did not matter nearly as much as previously thought. In the Reformation, the new church fathers returned to this tradition, giving up our very *selves* to the divine agency of God.

The revivalist fervor that swept Europe following the Reformation was echoed in the revivals of nineteenth-century America, where preachers like John Wesley, the founder of Methodism, were careful to distinguish between faith of the head versus faith of the heart. The heart is where true transformation takes place, while faith of the head is the force of will and does not lead to sincere or real change in the person as they submit to God. New life and faith are symbolized by changes within the person.

I journaled a lot when I was younger as part of my daily practice of devotionals. Most of those notebooks have been lost to time, but I have one from the summer after I graduated high school. I filled the little leatherbound journal from cover to cover with prayers and thoughts only a sheltered eighteen-year-old evangelical Christian could have. During that summer, I was trying to decide what I wanted to pursue in my life and opted to go into theology so I could become a preacher. As I was deciding, I journaled: "[God] reigns over all and He is more important than all. My life, whether I like it or not, is totally His. Completely in His control. He could pluck me off this earth at any point if He wanted to, yet he keeps me on." Looking back on this twenty years later, I recognize in myself a desire to control and subdue my own self in order that my belief in God could reign supreme. I would not and could not let myself be happy—every moment of happiness in that journal is immediately followed by regretful proclamations of my sinfulness in my flesh. Omri Elisha, an anthropologist at the City University of New York, points out that such proclamations of change are not, in fact embodiment or acknowledgment of the individual body as important. Instead, he writes in a 2008 study of an evangelical megachurch in Knoxville, Tennessee: "The crucial factor for most evangelical Protestants is the process of becoming the subject of divine volition (i.e., becoming faith*ful*), and thereby being endowed with qualities that are understood to originate from a divine source."[11] In other words, the body of the Christian does not maintain any individual identity but instead is a vessel, a jar of clay, a mechanism for God to pour out God's Spirit. As Elisha continues, "Conservative evangelicals share a view of humanity as inherently corrupted and incapable of doing anything of moral significance without the guidance of biblical and/or spiritual revelation. . . . It is suggestive of a radical reconstitution of the self that seeks as its outcome a life in which the will of God literally 'dwells' in the life and body of the believer."[12] In other words, within the body of the believer, the self, the essence of who we are, is replaced in submission to God. It is important here to note that evangelicals talk of this as though a new person has been born—a new life in Christ, a new birth. But as long as we dwell in these fleshy prisons, we will forever be tempted toward sin.

The body, then, is the ultimate barrier to a full union and understanding of God, and therefore, the body becomes an object to fear—a body that does not comply with the divine authority and agency, which does not easily bend to control, is a symptom of moral decay, of moral decadence, of rebellion. The fear that an uncontrolled body could keep one from the divine—and, in its natural state, according to the doctrine of total depravity, absolutely does so—is so terrifying that the only way to proceed is to turn the body into a tool, not a self. What body I inhabit matters less than what I *do* with that body.

Of course, any time there's a divergence between traditions, it is important to examine what is happening on either side of the divergence. Where Christianity went into a more ascetic and dualistic direction in distinguishing itself from Roman society, Jewish tradition largely hewed to its own centuries of understanding. Loosely explained, both by Jewish scholars and by my Jewish friends, but summarized well by scholar Daniel Boyarin in Carnal Israel: "Rabbinic Judaism . . . defined the human being as an animated body and not as a soul trapped or even housed or clothed in a body." Boyarin then quotes Alon Goshen-Gottsein: ". . . there is not a fundamental metaphysical opposition between these two aspects [of body and soul]. There may be an existential confrontation, but metaphysically soul and body form a whole, rather than a polarity."[13]

Instead of typical readings in Christianity, where the soul is a separate persona that uses a body to its ends, insofar as Jewish tradition talks about a soul, it discusses an animating force that makes the body function and is an integral part of the body itself. Soul is also referred to as a breath of life—that which forms the body is so tied together with that which animates it that the soul is the air we breathe, the unconscious, unseen, and automatic process of taking your next breath. In the evangelical Christianity I grew up in, the body and soul are constantly at war: my mind attempting to subdue my body. In the Jewish tradition I have dabbled in as I became disillusioned with

Christianity, I have learned that bodies exist as animated by and in the image of G-d—our bodies *are* our selves.

I started going to a weekly Torah study with friends in late 2022. I realized that in order to change my thinking about religion in the world, I needed to be exposed to how people of other faiths think. Luckily, I live in a metro area with a large and diverse population of Jewish people, and have many friends who were raised Jewish or converted later in life. I'd watched over the past few years as several friends found a home in Jewish thought, and while I'm still largely unaffiliated, I see why and how they were drawn to it. Learning about Jewish thought and tradition feels daunting—after all, my religious thinking has been trained and sculpted by evangelical Christianity, which strives to have an answer for any question and believes strongly that there are right or wrong answers to theological questions. In my experience with Torah and Talmud, however, Jewish people seem much more interested in the debate, in the discussion, in the overall ethic of life rather than staking their lives on tiny questions like whether or not to include drums in a service (though I'm sure somewhere Rabbis have written on and disagreed about it).

But I find myself most drawn to Jewish thought on the idea of the body. As a non-binary trans queer person, the idea that I'm simply an amorphous soul housed in a meat suit has never quite sat right with me. Back when I was still an evangelical, a friend asked me if I'd believe in the Christian God if I was born in, say, Afghanistan or China. The "I" that would be born in those circumstances would have no resemblance to the "I" born in Sioux Falls, South Dakota, on a cold February morning in the 1980s. I thought about this question over and over in the decades since, and I've realized that it's become a guiding principle for understanding my own sense of self. So much of what forms who we are and how we think is basically a circumstance of birth; our bodies are so vital and important in forming who we are that to say we would be the same person if born under completely different circumstances is an impossibility. Embracing that impossibility has helped me to embrace my body—the body that formed the "I" with which I refer to myself.

Yet American culture as a whole does not want to recognize that basic principle. And this divergence that started shortly after the time of Jesus has metastasized into a pernicious way of thinking that separates people from communities, denies their lived experiences, and elides difference in favor of treating everyone as though they are a white, cisgender, heterosexual man. We may not be a "Christian nation," but we are a nation and culture that struggles immensely with our cultural Protestantism imbued in whiteness coming into conflict with the pluralistic society we actually *are*. Dismantling this dualism of body and soul requires America itself to examine our history and our own soul as a country.

Perhaps the best and most corrupt example of this thinking emerged in 2019, when a local pastor here in Minneapolis decided to declare that empathy—the ability to share and experience another person's feelings alongside them—is a sin. Joe Rigney was, at the time, the pastor of Cities Church and President of Bethlehem College and Seminary, both of which are institutions in the evangelical world established by pastor John Piper, a neo-Calvinist Reformed pastor who runs a megachurch empire here in the Twin Cities metro area. In collaboration with Douglas Wilson, a pastor in Moscow, Idaho, who led protests against mask mandates during the pandemic, Rigney launched an offensive against the concept of "empathy" through both podcasts and follow-up writings from both pastors.

Writing in the style of C. S. Lewis's *Screwtape Letters*, wherein a demon sends letters to his underlings on how best to tempt Christians into sin (a popular device among white male Christian writers), Rigney informs his demon correspondent that "Compassion only suffers *with* another person; empathy suffers *in* them. It's a total immersion into the pain, sorrow, and suffering of the afflicted."[14] This is a sin, Rigney writes, because it requires that the one empathizing abandon truth to prioritize the other person, that one's theology must bend to the human experience. Feeling what other people are feeling as a means to understanding them, Rigney writes, is a problem because it tempts Christians away from capital-T Truth about God's word on sinfulness.

This refusal to entertain the lived experience of others, to potentially open oneself up to what it means to live in their body, is the logical endpoint of the evangelical rejection of the body. If the body does not matter, then the differing experience of humans with their bodies likewise does not matter, as that is merely an artifact of the sinful world in which we live. Bodies are, in this view, broken things that we must consistently compel with our habits toward good—a fundamentally negative view of flesh. Indeed, throughout evangelicalism, "the flesh" and "the spirit" are a dichotomy set against each other, and the good Christian is the one for whom the spirit has conquered the flesh.

All of this ties back into the political sphere. If the body is merely a tool to be molded, a thing to be subsumed to the greater power of the spirit, then any argument that prioritizes bodily experience, that emphasizes the importance of the body or even gives it priority, is necessarily false. As Butler argues in *White Evangelical Racism*, the evangelical movement regards the Black experience as one that must be subsumed into whiteness, as an experience of the body that must be subsumed into the spirit:

> The general expectation of white evangelicals in both the nineteenth and the twentieth centuries was that nonwhite believers would take on the practices and viewpoints of white members and leadership, no matter the cultural contexts in which Black evangelicals had been born or raised. As a result, tensions surrounding race and ethnicity commonly lodged in harsh criticism of Black cultural practices of dress, singing, or worship expressions. In order for Black evangelicals to belong, they had to emulate whiteness.[15]

And in the twenty-first century, this conception of the body as secondary, as merely a vessel for our souls, has driven politics around transgender communities and parents and the rights of children—a rallying cry that has been taken up even by the nonreligious right wing as the culture war rages. I'll discuss trans bodies in more depth in a later chapter, but the emphasis on children is worth considering here, as it is likewise a microcosm of their view of the body—and this theological influence in the culture wars has created an outsized impact, even as numbers of self-identified evangelicals dwindle.

My father and I do not talk. We haven't really spoken since Christmas of 2021, but the rift had started well before then when he revealed to me that, despite having a queer kid (me), he still believed that LGBT people are engaged in sin and could not be gay or queer or trans to be accepted by God. My brother and his family—his wife and two daughters—were appalled by this betrayal and chose to stand by me and limit contact with Dad as well. They also had had numerous disagreements on politics, as Dad had grown up as an evangelical Republican in the sixties and seventies, and his views hadn't changed much since.

It's Christmas tradition for me to drive to my brother's home in South Dakota and spend Christmas with them. That Christmas Eve in 2021, the last time I spoke to my dad, my brother stepped out to shovel the driveway and discovered our dad had dropped off a stack of presents for the family, so he obligingly brought them in and added them to the pile. The next morning, we went through opening the presents, with the two nieces—then eleven and five—getting the most: piles of toys and books and new fun make-up kits. Dad's presents were expected—one was actually a repeat of what he'd given the girls last year—and we were down to the last one. My older niece heaved the package up and noted it was addressed to both the girls. They ripped it open and stared in confusion at the pile of a dozen or so thin books that fell out.

I involuntarily gasped when I realized what the books were: the full collection of *The Tuttle Twins*, a conservative libertarian children's book series by Mormon writer Connor Boyack. The books—endorsed by conservative firebrands like Glenn Beck and Sean Hannity—are designed to teach children libertarian principles, like "let the market decide" and "government regulation is bad!"

It was the most passive aggressive present my father could've chosen. It was clearly meant as a dig at my brother and his wife's parenting—apparently he felt it important that my nieces get some "conservative perspectives" in their lives. It also made it clear what he thinks of children—rather than considering who his nieces are, and their own perspectives and ideas, he thought handing them what amounts to conservative propaganda would be useful. The message was clear: he believes that we are indoctrinating the girls into liberal thinking, so he wanted to "counter-balance."

This suspicion was confirmed a month later when my dad dropped by my brother's house and stood out in the cold garage talking with my brother for half an hour about why he sent those books along. He believed that my brother and his wife were, indeed, engaged in indoctrination and he wanted to counter-program his grandchildren. The idea that the girls are capable of making their own decisions, of being their own persons, did not enter into consideration at all. Those children were not human to him, not really, not fully, not people in their own right. They were tools in this broader culture war.

When we disconnect from our bodies sufficiently, we disconnect from our own humanity and that of others. In white evangelicalism, the child's mind is not fully formed, so they are not fully human yet. Ray Comfort, conservative evangelical and promoter of Creationism, talks about fathers not wanting to deal with their babies until they become "real" to them—that is, until the infant starts smiling back and demonstrating something of a personality. Comfort uses this colorful little idea to introduce a much more horrifying one: that the little child you are holding is a sinner and wants to rebel against you. Comfort writes: "So, reject the world's philosophy, and instead embrace the biblical viewpoint. Again, God's Word says that there is none good. Not one. Your child isn't good. He is like the rest of us. His heart is evil. Face the ugliness."[16]

Your child is not a human, evangelicalism tells us. Your child will become the next Jeffrey Dahmer if you do not embrace a righteous fear of the Lord. Fear of your own sinfulness. Fear of what God may do. Fear of how your own body may betray you. As Comfort tells us, even the infant demonstrates an instinct toward rebellion by how he arches his back when he is upset at being held or restrained.[17] The first assertion of our bodies as beings in their own rights, our first resistance against the guiding hands of a parent, is seen by the evangelical as the start of evil and sin. If the body is not forced to obey, if we are not brought in line to *fear*, then all is lost.

* * *

The driving force behind much of white America's approach to the body is fear. Bodies are objects to be feared, to be controlled, to be subdued. It is this fear that drives much of how we talk about the world in America—two perspectives coming into conflict, where our bodies are what matters, and where our bodies are what must be controlled. It is fear that drives much of America in our politics— fear that our bodies may betray us, fear that our bodies may one day wither and die, fear that control of our bodies may be stolen from us. That fear of who and what we are as material forms is the centerpiece of American culture that needs dismantling. The evangelical fear of the body is merely one part, one aspect. But it pervades how we see our very selves in everyday culture—as souls housed in electrified meat, not as bodies unto themselves. Even without believing directly in this theology, we still have it embedded in our culture, embedded in how we talk about other people, and how bodies of those who are different are controlled, criminalized, and condemned.

Even if you don't believe in a soul, the way other people do believe affects how they treat and understand you and your body. That fear, as we'll examine later, can end lives. But first we have to understand what that fear looks like.

2 | THE HUMAN BODY

Every teenager goes through a phase where they're learning that other people actually exist and have independent lives. Child development specialists call this a theory of other minds—you start realizing that other people actually do exist and are human like you. For a lot of teens, this development manifests in hyper-awareness of potential embarrassment. We want to disappear when we're out with our parents and they start doing things we believe to be embarrassing. We think the entire world is watching us move and judging and scolding us in their minds. Because the realization that other people are people is a new one for teenagers, they lack a real sense of proportion or recognition that while other people exist, they are not the vigilant judges we imagine them to be.

One part of that era that stuck with me well into adulthood was my own attentiveness, which I developed to compensate for my dad's inattentiveness. It seemed for him that he never fully developed a sense of other people existing within his physical space, and whenever we would go out together, I was constantly monitoring and telling him that he needed to move because other people were around and trying to get by him. "Spatial awareness, Dad," I'd say with an exasperated sigh after smilingly making excuses for him to yet another young mom with a toddler struggling to move her cart past him as he stood in the middle of the grocery aisle.

I've thought about this a lot more as an adult studying gender and how bodies move through space. My father never had to be aware of his presence in space because he simply expected other people to move for him. And I, designated female at birth, took on the role of being his spotter, watching out for his movements in public on his behalf. As I grew older and into a more feminist ethic, I realized that I had been protecting him from the reality of his own choices. So I stopped. I gave the burden of his bodily space back to him and stopped extending myself out to cover more of his space. But my anxiety made it very hard to do that.

I battled with my own body for a long time, though I didn't realize that was happening. From as far back as I can remember, I've been tortured by a brain that spirals out catastrophe at the smallest suggestion. I remember when my family would go for drives around the lake where my mom grew up; I'd see the edges of the road and the drop-off to the lake and begin panicking as, in my mind's eye, I saw our car slip off the edge and slide into the water. It never occurred to me that we were on a paved road driven by people every day and that my father, who had been driving since he was twelve, was more than capable of keeping the car on the road. Something in my brain convinced me that disaster was looming just around the corner, and I would begin to panic.

As a teenager, the anxiety turned inward. I obsessed over whether or not I was doing religion right, begging forgiveness for allowing myself to exist in my body. By the time I made it to college, I'd been to the doctor with mysterious stomachaches and alleged flus that never showed any symptoms other than a constant fear that I was going to vomit at an inopportune moment. No one at any point examined my psychological state, suggested that it could be something in my head— had that been said, I might've been able to get a diagnosis earlier and my body wouldn't have become so completely alien to me.

I disconnected from my body well into my twenties, as a combination of the culture in which I was raised and my anxiety disorder made it impossible for me to understand myself. At twenty-five, I realized I had anxiety, but it took me another three years before I would actually seek help for it. And now, over a decade later, on medication and more comfortable with my gender and sexuality, I finally feel somewhat integrated into my body. But it took a very long time for me to arrive here. I also realized that I couldn't simply blame the disconnect on anxiety. While my body had become an enemy for an extended period of time—something foreign to me, dictating how my days would go—I realized, too, that I was struggling with the feeling of being *marked*, *different*.

In feminist theory, there's a fairly simple concept about who gets to be considered the default in society and who is otherwise *marked*. The idea of being marked or unmarked is a guiding principle in understanding power structures and invisible oppressions, ways in which society reinforces the boundaries of behavior and ideas. To explain the concept, let us draw an example from legal framing.

In law, the concept known as the reasonable person standard is a method for evaluating behavior, often in cases of negligence. If a defendant in a case acted in a manner considered reasonable for the average person, then they are not necessarily culpable for actions they took that were reasonable. Here's an example: just after this book sold, I was driving in Minneapolis in a carshare car (rental cars rented by the hour, instead of the day). I stopped at a red light and moved forward when it turned green. I looked to my left and saw a gray Jeep Grand Cherokee pause at the red light and then accelerate toward me. I honked the horn, slammed on the brakes, and tried to turn the car so I wouldn't get T-boned directly. The jeep slammed into the driver's side front wheel well, knocking the wheel entirely off the axle, and tossing me around like a rag doll in the driver's seat. I got out and called 911, only to turn around and see the Jeep driving off, after its driver had paused to check that their own car was drivable.

I was taken to the hospital in an ambulance to have my shoulder x-rayed and spent the next month dealing with paperwork to ensure that the bills were all paid. A police officer took a report and a description of the vehicle, though nothing seemed to actually come of it. Had we tracked down the driver of the other car, the rental car company would've had standing to sue them for liability for damages because they did not act in a reasonable manner when operating a motor vehicle—the reasonableness here being that one would obey traffic laws and not cause injury to others. Accelerating to beat another car through an intersection is not acting in a reasonable manner under the law.

But had the driver's brakes failed, causing them to run a red light and cause an accident, the accident would've been considered no-fault, or as "pure" an accident as you can have. Had the driver attempted to stop (and obey the law) but was unable to do so because of a mechanical failure, that would mitigate liability in such a case, under the reasonable person standard. If a person is otherwise behaving reasonably and something happens that is outside of their control, they are often considered, under the law, not to be liable for the results of what happened. This is the reasonable person standard.

But feminist legal scholars have noticed problems with this standard when it comes to cases involving people possessing different identities, where the case and liability are predicated on those identities. In cases of sexual harassment, scholars have long argued for a reasonable *woman* standard that takes into account power dynamics between men and women regarding whether or not a workplace behavior was necessarily harassment or constituted creating a hostile work environment under the law. The standard was developed out of a 1991 ruling from the Ninth Federal Appellate Court, which rejected a case precedent previously set in 1986 where the court had decided that in "assessing a workplace sexual harassment claim, a court 'must adopt the perspective of a reasonable person's reaction to a similar environment.'"[1] Five years later, the court of appeals ruled that the standard that must be used in these cases should consider the social dynamics between men and women and adopt, instead, a reasonable *woman* standard—what a man might consider reasonable and routine is likely separate and different from a woman in the same situation, therefore the reasonable woman standard was necessary. Such a stance asks judges and juries to adopt the viewpoint of the victim in such cases (the majority of which are women) and to understand how a reasonable *victim* might respond.[2]

Circling back around: this is the legal application of the feminist theory of marked versus unmarked. Men are considered the default in the law and so when thinking about a reasonable person, very often gender, race, sexuality, and ability do not enter into the equation. But as the court noticed three decades ago, the application of a gender-neutral "reasonable" standard actually perpetuates further harm because it causes people who are not cisgender, heterosexual men to face a higher burden in proving their case—for example, a reasonable woman would react poorly to a male colleague following her into a dark parking lot at night, while a male colleague might not give it a second thought. This is the idea of marked and unmarked— anyone not a cishet white man is marked by their deviation from that standard.

In 2010, shortly after graduating from Baylor University, I hopped on a plane to Tokyo and then on a connecting flight to the city of Fukuoka, where I would begin my new life in Japan. I'd been hired to be an English teacher at a Methodist university in Shimonoseki, a city of around 300,000 people that sits on the Kanmon Strait between the big island of Honshu and the southern island of Kyushu. It was there that I experienced true mental friction at being no longer considered the default. Everything about moving through the world became just a little bit harder. I tried going to church with a friend, but it was a twenty-minute train ride into a different town, and while the pastor provided English translations of his message, the entire service was in Japanese.

Going into stores, I would be greeted by the shrill welcoming sound of the shop clerks: "OHAIOGOZIMAS!" at the top of their lungs, a sensory experience unlike any I'd had before. I found myself going into American fast food stores because at least there I could point to an item on the menu and know approximately what I was going to get. Riding public transit meant being stared at by young children who had never seen a white person before and adults attempting to try out their English on me. In one memorable instance, a forty-something-year-old man decided he wanted to show off his martial arts skills to me in the aisle on a moving train, explaining that he runs a school for karate in town and had visited America to teach karate. I had no idea how to communicate to him or make him stop kicking at air on the train as other people stared at me as though I was the cause of this outburst—and in a way, I was. My presence in their midst had somehow elicited this display, and that made me a disturbance.

I was a white person in a world that was not built with me as the default. I did not speak Japanese and of course did not read it. I learned the symbols I needed to, recognizing the little house symbol for my city, "Shimonoseki" (下関市), and the three lines that symbolized the mountains for Yamaguchi, the prefecture where I lived (山口県). In the 7–11 on the way home, I memorized the symbols for "salmon" (鮭) so I could find salmon onigiri, the triangle-shaped hand roll of sushi that was a daily snack on my way home from work. When I took a Shinkansen (bullet train) to Tokyo, I spent an uncomfortable five hours in a train seat that was too small, with no place to put my long American legs. I later told a friend that it was a hard lesson that Japanese trains are not built for American rear ends unless you upgrade to the plush seats in first class.

In this pre-smartphone era, every venture outside my house was a mental and physical toll on my body—what happened if I got lost? What happened when I couldn't communicate?

It was constant mental friction from existing in a body that was outside the norm for the area in which I existed. I understood in those ten months I lived there that I could no longer assume that others had the same experiences as me, that my life was in any way a default, that my *mind* was somehow unique in the world. Here I existed in an entire nation of people different from me, whose inner lives and ways of communicating were so far removed from my own that conflict and miscommunication were inevitable. I was marked, in a way different from what I was accustomed to—so totally and completely foreign to the society in which I existed.

The separation of the mind and the body into distinct categories, with the mind as primary, doesn't exactly work in a world where people are different from each other. The idea that we are mind stuff and our bodies are merely meat suits only works if the meat suits don't matter and the mind stuff isn't shaped by the experiences of the meat suit. René Descartes, who was one of the primary philosophers proposing dualism as an answer to how the material world works, had the liberty to assume that his body did not matter, because the impacts it had on who he was were made invisible to him. My whiteness was invisible to me until I ventured into spaces where I was made a minority—where my default was now the difference. Suddenly my body became all that mattered.

Reconciling the brain and the body has been an ongoing field of study for literally centuries. We are functionally brains, existing in these weird flesh suits with appendages and somehow interacting with the physical world. Scientists, philosophers, and stoners at 3 a.m. have worked hard to try to answer the question. I'm not proposing that I have the answer to this problem of what, exactly, we are, but rather a lens for examining both the cultural impact of separating out "soul," mind, and body and the importance of integrated, whole bodies, with a little help from disability studies.

First, let's walk through a couple of the different perspectives.

One of the foremost questions of philosophy as a field is asking "what *are* we?" Dualism (again, proposed by Descartes) is the idea that the mind, in a non-physical existence, can be separate from the body. The *substance* of the two are distinct—the mind does not inhabit space but is rather something *else* entirely, a different substance from this physical space that is what we experience interpreted through our minds. The "brain" is not the residence of the mind but merely part of the physical substance that is "matter."

For dualists, the mind is primary and the body is secondary in terms of importance. American tradition tends to hold to this as a cultural standard, equating the mind with a soul or a spirit, as something other than the body a person inhabits. We invoke this dualism in how we talk about our bodies in the everyday—churches talk of sins of the flesh and songwriters talk of the conflict between the heart and the mind. Much of this dualism can be tied back to the influence of Protestant theology, as explained in chapter 1, but also to an American culture of meritocracy, where the person who has the best *mind* and works the smartest is considered worthy of respect. We value the mind as an amorphous representation of who a person is while ignoring their body and its location in the world.

In contrast, philosophy also brings us materialism. You may have come across the idea of materialism before, especially if you're familiar with trans issues—Kathleen Stock is a materialist and uses materialism as the basis for her critique of transgender identity (more on that in chapter 6). Materialism is the idea that the fundamental substance from which everything is built is simply *matter* (as in "mind over . . ." not as in "black lives . . ."). In philosophy a lot of hubbub is made of the order of things, the order of the universe. For idealists—the contrasting method of thought to materialists—mind and conscious-ness are first order ideals and matter is arranged around those. Mate-rialism, on the other hand, proposes that mind and consciousness arise from the warm soup that is matter and that they cannot exist without the physical structures. Whatever this thing called "mind" is, it is deeply and irrevocably tied to the physical structures that exist.

The implications of this are obvious: there is no such thing as a soul, or a part of the self that can exist aside from or apart from the physical body. The *supernatural* is impossible because there is nothing that can go above or beyond the natural. And bodies, therefore, are deeply important in that they are all we get, all we are.

For many, the idea that there is nothing beyond our physical selves is terrifying. It can also bring in questions of free will—if all we are is electrified meat, just these bodies, then what, if anything, is consciousness? Are we actually aware or are we just working out a predetermined path based on what our neurons in our brain meat are firing that day? Are we born this way or do we have a say in who we become? To what extent are minds even *real?*

But the social categories also bring up challenges for materi-alism, because putting matter as the first order ahead of the mind creates challenges for the sheer complexity of human society. There's a tendency to use materialism—or at least that which claims to be a version of it—to rely on a form of biological determinism to argue that if something has a biological basis or is biologically differentiated, like skin color, then the meanings and behaviors and habits we ascribe to those aspects must also be true. But materialism does not actually go that far—while "matter acting upon matter" is a primary basis for eventual theories of determinism, materialism itself does not demand that we ascribe such meanings to matter. Matter is the primary form of the universe, and what we take that to *mean* is a separate question. Materialism simply answers the question of "what is reality and how did it come about" with one word: "matter."

There's a lot more to both perspectives but I've summarized essentially what's relevant here. It's important, too, to note that medicine and science tend to support a more complex materialist view of how we function in the universe. Changing physical structures in the brain can result in deep and lasting changes in how a person both views themselves and behaves in the world—it literally changes their mind.

In 1848, Phineas Gage was working on a railroad construction project in Vermont, using high-powered explosives to blow away a section of rock so the train could cut through the mountain. Explosives at the time weren't just a stick of dynamite—a mostly stable container for explosive material that has to be ignited—but loose powder that is shoved down into a hole, packed with sand, and then lit via fuse. The powder and sand had to be tamped down into the hole using a large iron bar. On that particular September day, Gage had neglected to put the protective layer of sand in the hole before he began tamping down the powder. In a moment of distraction, Gage looked up and over at his crew, and the tamping iron scraped against the rock just enough to spark. The subsequent explosion shot the iron rod through Gage's face, entering just under his left cheekbone, up through the eye socket, and out the top of his head. The bar landed around eighty feet away.

Gage fell to the ground, seized for a little bit, but according to witness accounts, was up and talking again within a few minutes. He even sat up the entire ride in the back of an ox cart to get to help. Doctors who saw him at first could not believe that he had taken such a blow and was still talking. In one of the first reports on the case, in the *American Journal of Medical Sciences* published in 1850, physicians who saw Gage soon after the accident testified that "the pulsations of the brain being very distinct," Gage later became ill and violently threw up, resulting in "about a half teacupful of the brain"[3] being pressed out through his wound and onto the floor.

But the entire time his brain was literally falling onto the floor, Gage was up and speaking and talking rationally. Repairs were made to the wound as best could be done at the time, with Gage sedate and almost comatose for much of the time. By Halloween of that year, however, he had recovered nearly fully, and after getting through some infection in November, was essentially back to normal by Christmas.

Well, normal-ish. A contemporaneous account from his doctor relays what Gage's coworkers and loved ones said about his behavior. Prior to the accident, he was responsible, rational, and hardworking, much loved by the men on his crew. After, the doctor explains:

> The equilibrium or balance, so to speak, between his intellectual faculties and animal propensities, seems to have been destroyed. He is fitful, irreverent, indulging at times in the grossest profanity (which was not previously his custom), manifesting but little deference for his fellows, impatient of restraint or advice when it conflicts with his desires, at times pertinaciously obstinate, yet capricious and vacillating, devising many plans of future operations, which are no sooner arranged than they are abandoned in turn for others appearing more feasible. A child in his intellectual capacity and manifestations, he has the animal passions of a strong man. Previous to his injury, although untrained in the schools, he possessed a well-balanced mind, and was looked upon by those who knew him as a shrewd, smart business man, very energetic and persistent in executing all his plans of operation. In this regard his mind was radically changed, so decidedly that his friends and acquaintances said he was "no longer Gage."[4]

His personality changed so fundamentally that his friends and family no longer recognized him as the same person. Particularly, he lacked impulse control, and was prone to fits of anger that shocked his compatriots.

Gage's case was the first of many cases in which the dualism of the mind existing outside the body was challenged. Early neuroscience realized, from Gage's case and other studies, that removal of sections of the prefrontal cortex resulted in extreme personality changes, such that a person could be said not to resemble the person they were before the change. Science taught us that damage to specific parts of the brain could fundamentally change how a person interacted with the world. We don't have first-person testimony from Gage as to how *he* saw himself after the change, but we know that the change was such that others who knew him well felt that he was an entirely different person.

If the mind really is some otherworldly substance, unaffected by the physical realm, how then, can a change in the brain so deeply affect a person's mind? It seems improbable that dualism is actually a supportable conclusion, but that hasn't stopped American culture from operating as though dualism is right and true.

All of this really comes down to one question: "what in the hell *is* consciousness?" What does it *mean* to exist in this physical world and to have the self-awareness to know and think about the fact that we are brains thinking about ourselves? It's pretty freaky when you give it any thought, which is probably why it's been a part of philosophical thought ever since . . . well, ever since we started thinking.

I believed for a long time that our minds are a kind of thing handed down to us by our Creator, our personalities and selves formed perfectly by God in the womb. But life has taught me otherwise. It's easy to assume that you are who you are because of some mystical process when everyone around you shares the same basic upbringing and experience. But all it takes is a bit of getting outside that narrow sphere to realize that who you are is an artifact of all you have encountered and seen and understood. I was lucky early on to be able to travel the world and encounter a number of people whose lives and experiences are different from mine, shaping who I am as I rolled into their spaces like a grocery cart bumping into my oblivious father in the grocery store aisle.

But even as an evangelical, I knew in my gut that our physical circumstances, our physical bodies, do one hell of a lot to shape who we are. My oldest brother has Down syndrome. Down syndrome is caused by an extra chromosome on the twenty-first pair of chromosomes in a human's twenty-three pairs of chromosomes that determine how our bodies form. My brother was born in 1982, just two short years after the United States officially ended the mandatory institutionalization of people with disabilities. Prior to 1980, it was common practice that a child born with intellectual or developmental disabilities—like Down syndrome—would be whisked off to an institution or a group home to be raised by strangers and separated from society forever. Thanks to a parents' movement in Minnesota that started in the 1940s, the United States eventually ended this barbaric practice, making it more possible for children to stay home with their families and integrate into the regular school system. The argument was twofold: people with disabilities are still people who deserve dignity, human rights, and full participation in society, and, second, society as a whole benefits from being heterogeneous, not homogeneous.

With my brother at my side through childhood, I understood his world to be shaped entirely by the limitations and formations of his body. Because of the circumstances of his birth, of the body in which he was born, his sense of self and the world around him was different from the white, abled norm. Down syndrome is both a physical and mental disability—people with Down syndrome have a very specific facial structure with small, slanted eyes, a narrow mouth, and a larger than normal tongue. These physical characteristics affect speech development, often making it harder for people with the syndrome to be understood when speaking. As a child, I frequently acted as a translator for my brother, able to interpret his unique way of speaking that my parents sometimes misunderstood.

Shortly after he was born, a stranger approached my mother at church one Sunday and asked if she could pray for my mom to be rid of whatever unresolved sin she had in her life that had caused her to bear such a child. This incident, my mom told me decades later, changed my mother's perspective on church forever. Her son, whom she had carried for nine months and for whom she was learning to care, was not a product of sinfulness or unworthiness. He was simply who he was. That's all.

It was disability studies that eventually gave me the term necessary to discuss this conception—that our physical bodies and our minds are not two different theoretical constructs but are fully linked and inextricable composition of the *self*. Sami Schalk, a professor of Gender and Women's Studies at the University of Wisconsin in Madison, has written prolifically about the intersection of race, ability, and sexuality. In her 2018 book, *Bodyminds Reimagined*, she examines the positioning of disability in Black women's speculative fiction, exploring how disability is embraced and rejected and understood in texts ranging from Octavia Butler's to contemporary television series. A central concept in her work—one that pervades disability justice activism and academic disability studies—is the concept of the "bodymind." She describes "bodymind" as follows:

> Bodymind is a materialist feminist disability studies concept from Margaret Price that refers to the enmeshment of the mind and the body, which are typically understood as interacting and connected, yet distinct entities due to the Cartesian dualism of Western Philosophy. The term *bodymind* insists on the inextricability of mind and body and highlights how processes within our being impact one another in such a way that the notion of a physical versus mental process is difficult, if not impossible to clearly discern in most cases. . . . The term bodymind can help highlight the relationship of nonphysical experiences of oppression—psychic stress—and overall well-being.[5]

In order to truly understand other humans, treating them neither as simply bodies nor simply minds is vital. Separating the body from the mind is impossible, scientifically and metaphysically, so we do not bother. We are and exist as bodyminds, an interlinked and unbreakable physical and metaphysical object, all at once. Who we are as disabled people is who we *are*. There is not some magical universe in which a non-disabled version of my brother exists. And if his disabled body is who he is, then my abled, queer, trans one is me as well. We are material existing in a physical plane, shaped by our physical forms and our experiences.

And now I see how much damage the dualist vision of soul inhabiting a body has done to those I love and to broader American culture. The dualistic view that the flesh does not matter, that we are brains in flesh-shaped jars, has been the source of our cultural phobias, from homophobia, to transphobia, to fatphobia, to ableism and all other prejudices that boil down to the fear that someone being different is a threat to who another person is. It is time, then, to embrace more of those perspectives that take the body seriously and understand it as the essence of our very self. Our cultural anxiety about the flesh, born of Protestant theology turned justification for capitalist greed, needs to be confronted head on and challenged for what it is: fear of the other, fear of the self, and fear of being mortal. We will not get past all other phobias and prejudice until we confront culture's most central phobia: our bodies and our selves.

3 | THE FAT BODY

In 2018, I wasn't sleeping well. I was waking myself up with my own snoring, and I couldn't seem to actually rest. At work, I was downing at minimum three cups of coffee every morning just to last through the day. I was exhausted all the time. On weekends, when I could sleep in, I frequently found myself asleep until noon or later, and I'd still be tired. I'd also gained a lot of weight within the last couple of years and was working with my doctor to try to lose some in order to avoid potential health complications she believed would come with a higher weight.

I brought up my sleep problems with my doctor and mentioned specifically that I wanted to get a sleep study because I have a family history of sleep apnea—both my brothers and my father have it and have used CPAPs (continuous positive airway pressure machine) to help them sleep at night. Sleep apnea is a condition where your airway collapses as you sleep, causing you to stop breathing and then gasp awake several times in an hour. This cycle prevents the deep, restorative REM sleep that makes sleep truly fully restful, and the condition runs in families, so I knew that if I was tired all the time, it was a likely culprit.

My doctor in 2018 disagreed. She asked me if my girlfriend had noted anything weird about my sleep, as sleep apnea is usually noticed first by partners who hear the gasping breaths in the middle of the night. My partner at the time and I only shared a bed about once a week, and she'd not mentioned anything. When I said that to my doctor, she said "then it's probably not sleep apnea. Let's concentrate on losing weight then."

Fast forward to 2022. I hadn't lost the weight—indeed, I had lost fifteen pounds and then regained twice that. I was a week away from my first ever surgery, and I had to get approved by a doctor to know what potential problems could complicate anesthesia. So I went in and my blood pressure—after years and years of being extremely regular—popped high on the diastolic pressure, which is the second number in the formula for blood pressure. We retested and retested, and I begged my doctor to approve me for surgery anyway, saying that I could resolve the blood pressure issue later on. It was probably an unwise move, but I needed this surgery. I'd already made all the plans to take off work, and my friends had taken days off to help me recover. Eventually she relented and gave approval, as long as my blood pressure was in a reasonable position on the morning of the surgery. I managed to calm myself enough the morning of that the nurse said we could go through.

I learned, in that time when I was begging my doctor to allow me to go through with the surgery, that a high diastolic number is indicative of undiagnosed, long-term sleep apnea. After I'd recovered from surgery, my doctor put me on blood pressure medicine and got me scheduled for a sleep study. Sure enough, there it was: I stopped breathing between fourteen and twenty times in an hour over the course of the night. I got a CPAP and now sleep with a plastic mask under my nose to push humidified air into my airway at night, allowing me to sleep better. The difference has been life changing— I don't struggle to wake up anymore, I've reduced my coffee intake considerably, I'm no longer needing to lay down in the afternoon and nap.

For a long time, sleep apnea has been associated with weight—it tended to be diagnosed in people who have a higher number on the body mass index (BMI), which is a population level number derived by dividing a person's weight (in pounds) by the square of their height (in inches). This formula pops out a number usually between 15 and 50, and from there, it is compared to a population level of "normal," "underweight," and "overweight." Most people with sleep apnea tend to have a higher BMI, and many researchers over the years have theorized that weight causes sleep apnea as a result of excess fat around the throat, causing the airway to collapse. This is based on a cohort study out of the University of Wisconsin at Madison in 2005. This is the analysis my doctor in 2018 was relying on when she instructed me to lose weight as an answer to my sleep problems.[1]

In 2018, I was a newly fat person. Growing up, I'd always been the skinny kid—I weighed 110 pounds soaking wet when I graduated from high school and had been slowly adding weight as I got older. But then I turned thirty and gained around 70 pounds in a year. And it was also then that I started to literally wake myself up snoring. I was embarrassed by this new self—I had changed so drastically in the course of just a few months that I struggled with buying clothes that were the proper size, and I didn't want to accept that clothing that had fit me just a year before no longer did. I distanced myself from my body even more than I already had, unable to confront my own fear of being this thing that our culture so despised. I lamented, too, that I had only come to know myself as a queer person after I had passed the Rubicon from skinny, traditionally attractive woman into what felt like, to me, a fat blob stacked on a couple sticks for legs.

So when my doctor brought up losing weight as a solution to my sleep problems and potential other issues, I embraced it. I changed my diet. I counted steps. I worked hard to lose the fifteen pounds I did lose. And then winter came, seasonal depression set in, and I could not justify the cost of the health food I was consuming. I also started dating a person who was in recovery from an eating disorder, and it felt ethically and morally wrong to be counting calories when that was the thing that had destroyed her. I settled into my size, switched doctors to one who didn't attribute every issue to my weight, and learned to cook. I soon realized I had never been more at home in my body than when I embraced my non-binary gender, my fat body, and started working on simply having the energy to get through the day. When I got diagnosed with sleep apnea, more puzzle pieces fell into place.

Turns out, sleep apnea actually might cause weight gain. Apnea happens most often because of a genetic anomaly in the shape of a person's throat, where the tongue doesn't necessarily stay in the throat during sleep and instead can fall back and obstruct the airway. When this starts happening, sleep is no longer restorative, leading to health complications and making it much harder for a person to engage in activities that would maintain a specific weight—like an exercise regime. Additionally, the literal act of stopping breathing in the middle of the night can shift appetite, making a person hungrier during the day.

At the end of the day, what my doctor had prescribed me as a solution for a sleep problem was actually a prescription for a symptom of the illness rather than the illness itself. This, I realized, was my first encounter on a personal level with medical fatphobia—a bigotry where a doctor fails to look at underlying issues and simply blames a patient's weight for such problems. It is part of the objectification and vilification of the fat body, one which is not unique to American culture but is especially prevalent in our fear of the body.

In a 2007 study, researchers in New Zealand conducted a series of studies on how English-speaking cultures tend to frame fatness in moral terms. In three different forms, they collected how various populations that formed a cross-section of New Zealanders talk about and implicitly and cognitively judge fatness. Over and over throughout each study, they found that "the use of moral evaluative language is not simply interchangeable with more standard evaluative terminology. . . . Obesity is not just a disease that is caused by overeating and lack of exercise but one that is perceived as being caused by a moral failing of the individual to be 'good' to themselves."[2]

This language entering our common vocabulary as a culture is perhaps the easiest demonstration of how fear and condemnation of the body have seeped into the wider culture—the language of *sin* is inseparable from Protestant conceptions of the body. Discourse about bodies is clearest in the discourse around obesity, and the fear of the body is never more plain than here. Being fat is seen as a literal betrayal of one's body, an offensive and impious way of existing in the world. Even if an individual does not profess—or even explicitly rejects—Christian belief, the language often used to express fatphobia will fall into religious and moral terms. A cultural understanding of fat as an immoral act on the part of the fat person has deep, deep roots in white Anglo-Saxon Protestant culture in early America. The way we as an American culture talk about bodies in the here and now, in 2023, has its roots in the Protestant metaphysical debates of the late nineteenth century; the language from discussions of morality and sin have leached into the culture as improperly disposed of waste leaches into groundwater, making the body discussion a moral one rather than just accepting bodies as central to existence. And, historically, it's as American as apple pie.

America in the 1800s was, in a word, tumultuous. As the nation fought a war over whether or not it was appropriate to enslave other humans based on their race, white Christians felt their cultural control challenged—Black people were demonstrating their capacity for power, and white Christianity demanded subservience to hegemonic power. At the same time, the Third Great Awakening was shouting revival across the land, emphasizing social involvement for Christians as a mechanism for bringing out the Second Coming of Christ. Once social spheres were bent toward God, proponents of this Protestant revival argued, Christ would return and redeem the earth with his kingdom. With this renewed emphasis on godliness and social action, white women in the church who had been traditionally marginalized began to look for ways to garner power and show themselves on equal footing with men. And the way one achieved social power was through exhibiting control over one's body.

In previous centuries, over in mainland Europe, fatphobia wasn't necessarily a thing—fatness was actually associated positively with health, in that being skinny meant you lacked food and likely were poor and unable to survive. Fat was also associated with wealth and power—if you had enough food that you managed to get fat, it was reasoned, then you were wealthy and had access to health care and early medicine and could likely survive better. But in the 1700s, warnings about fatness began to take hold—not from a health angle but from a religious one. Being overweight was shifting toward being a sign of lack of self-control, overindulgence, and flaunting immorality. An overindulgent appetite for food was symbolized in culture to be part and parcel of an overindulgence in other appetites, particularly sexual, which signaled an immoral heart. Dieting became the prescribed response both for medical problems and for moral symbols of godliness.[3]

This English moralization of fat made its way onto American shores and eventually became embedded in American images of white masculine culture, drawing stark opposition to soft feminine curves. With the rise of the Civil War and an increased insecurity for white Christian men in the political sphere, threatened both by racial equality and the rise in gender equality movements like the suffragettes, white men began to moralize their bodies as a locus of control and power. A slender man, active, muscular, and fit, became the masculine ideal. Later on, white women began to adopt similar dieting tactics in order to assert their position in the racial hierarchy. But this move, too, was uniquely tied to the concept of Christian temperance.

In the late nineteenth century, women's movements began to take hold, one of which was the temperance movement. Alcoholism was a problem that plagued the lives of women as their husbands drank and often became abusive. The Women's Christian Temperance Union (WCTU) was founded in the 1870s and defined itself by calls to moderation of all harmful things and *healthful* things. Such calls marked a renewal of a Christian asceticism, a denial of the body exhibited by control of various appetites, including sexual and dietary. Control of the body in such a way has long been associated with a form of particularly Protestant Godliness, as reformer John Calvin articulated the practice of fasting as "a necessary discipline for appeasing God's wrath."[4] Temperance, then, meant both prohibition of alcohol and proper restraint in what one ate. Culturally, weight turned into a form of visible sinfulness.

R. Marie Griffith, a historian of evangelicalism in America, wrote about how the body was perceived during this time period in her 2004 book, *Born Again Bodies*. It is in this time period that we get the rise of Christian Science, founded by Mary Baker Eddy, who maintained that the body exists as a "sometimes beautiful, always erroneous delusion."[5] Many of Eddy's followers later summed up the principled denial of the body as based entirely in fear. Thomas Simmons, a man who was raised in Christian Science and later wrote a memoir about his experiences, is summed up by Griffith: "Underlying the ceaseless assurances of freedom, Simmons writes, was simply fear. 'We were afraid of everything—afraid of sickness, afraid of deviating from God's word, afraid of mortal mind, afraid of the body, afraid of sex, afraid of people, of difference, of strangers, even of love.'"[6]

Christian Science, of course, is an offshoot of Protestantism, and one cannot conflate the instances of Christian Science being abusive with Protestantism as a whole. But the center of thought—the denial of the body—was not unique to Christian Science in itself. Such thought emerged from a metaphysical movement of the late nineteenth century, one called New Thought, which was deeply important for how Americans viewed the body within religious lenses throughout the twentieth century. New Thought ideals about the body would be burnished down, sanitized, and brought to bear in more mainstream cultural spheres by 1950. Griffith expounds on this influence:

> Marginal as an organized movement by midcentury, New Thought filtered its suppositions about thought power shaping physical reality through elite sectors of American society then and later, including religious groups (evangelicals, among others) who had little else in common with such reputedly crackpot ideologies but who turned out to be, on similar albeit not identical grounds, stalwart defenders of beautiful bodies. Such concerns, we well know, were by no means limited to some sphere narrowly defined as the religious: America's manic pursuit of health that New Thought served and intensified until the activity became its own supposed type of religion still echoes the old theme of body as dangerous yet revelatory of purity and perfection, or else filth and decay. Elusively, but by no means insubstantially, New Thought played a key role in helping assemble the framework within which the bodily preoccupations of later Americans would take shape.[7]

By the mid-twentieth century, weight had been inextricably weaved together with the image of a good and righteous person. Presbyterian minister Charlie W. Shedd wrote in 1957: "We fatties are the only people on earth who can weigh our sin."[8] Fat became a shorthand for uncontrolled sinfulness—Shedd wrote one of the first of what would become many diet books in Christian culture, called *Pray the Weight Away.* Many believers at the time had begun incorporating the idea that the perception of health is of chief importance for believers, meaning that bodies must conform to a specific ideal as a reflection of one's spiritual state. As Shedd wrote: "When God first dreamed you into creation, there weren't 100 pounds excess avoirdupois [note: a measurement of weight] hanging around your belt. No, nor sixty, nor sixteen."[9] Diet culture hit the Christian world with the same force that the Great Awakening had done a century prior, reifying the sense of denial of the body and the flesh into a conception of fat as unholy.

When we arrive at the 2000s, weight loss and diet have become firmly ensconced in church life. Numerous pastors have written diet books, like Rick Warren's *The Daniel Plan*, Ted Haggard's *Jerusalem Diet*, or Tilly Dillehay's *Broken Bread*. Scrolling through church websites and popular evangelical blogs, one could easily take away the idea that having a *healthy* body is part and parcel of God's plan for you as a human being. In one memorable piece from John Piper's *Desiring God* ministry, Scott Hubbard writes that overeating—synonymous with fat—is a sin that recalls the original sin of Adam and Eve: "Food problems . . . go back to the beginning. Our own moments before the refrigerator or cupboard can, in some small measure, reenact that moment by the tree [in the Garden of Eden]."[10] The sin of fatness, of having a non-normative body, is linked to the original sin that doomed all mankind to hell.

I grew up with parents who were constantly battling their weight. My own journey reflects my mom's, who, after getting married and having children, put on weight and spent the next twenty years trying to lose it again. While I didn't have children, I started gaining weight when I hit my thirties, and I had to get used to taking up more room and checking weight limits on chairs, lest I embarrassingly collapse them. I remember my parents subscribing to Richard Simmons, Atkins' diet, and various other versions of diets that limited what they could eat and how often. And I know she felt guilty at not being able to lose the pounds.

At one family reunion, I found my mom crying in our A-frame cabin by a lake in Wisconsin where our extended family had rented space for the week. My dad is one of seven, and while most of the cousins of my generation were still young, all seven of the aunts and uncles would bring their families together for a reunion each summer.

Someone—I don't know who—would arrange to get t-shirts printed reading "Anderson Family Reunion" with the year emblazoned on it.

The year I found my mom crying, we had rented cabins in a row somewhere in northern Wisconsin, along a lake where we could go fishing and ride jet skis and have campfires. One afternoon we had gotten together to take a family picture. This was a production, with nineteen cousins, seven aunts and uncles and their spouses, and a couple grandparents. Several of my older cousins had brought their significant others, too. Coordinating around forty people for one photo was always a rough time, and making sure we were all wearing the same outfit meant ordering shirts weeks in advance and ensuring all the sizes were correct. That year, whoever ordered the shirts had made a mistake. They didn't order any sizes larger than a 1X, which fit nearly every one of the adults—except my mother, who wore a 2 or a 3X in most clothing brands. My aunt had suggested she try to "squeeze" into a 1X, a feat my mother's body would not allow. So my mom had to take the photos in what she had been wearing that day: a bright yellow shirt and jeans. The shirts that year were gray and blue, so Mom stuck out like a sore thumb. She was deeply embarrassed, and angry, because the lack of accommodation for her fat body felt like punishment. She felt alienated from the family despite having been married to my father for over twenty years at that point.

My mom consistently felt like she took up too much space. She hated having attention drawn to her and hated having to ask for accommodation for her body. During the last year of her life, when she was in and out of the hospital, I watched her apologize over and over to nurses and orderlies and doctors who were simply doing their jobs, simply trying to do the things that kept her alive. I always got the impression that she viewed having a body as a great inconvenience, which was why there was some relief in her when she informed the doctors she would no longer be pursuing treatment and instead opting for hospice.

I wish my mom's vision of herself could have been better. I don't know that she would've come around to *loving* her body, per se, but perhaps she would've, eventually, accepted that it is who she is, that her body made her who she was.

But it's hard when we live in a world that so deeply imbues us with hatred of our own flesh, even—and perhaps especially—as a spiritual discipline. John Piper, founder of one of the Twin Cities' local megachurches, responded to an anonymous woman who asked him for advice about how to stop hating her body. Piper responded first by looking to the Apostle Paul's words about disciplining his body, and then said, "Instead of saying 'I should stop hating my body' maybe I should say 'I should start hating my body in the right way; I should start hating my body because it tempts me to sin.'"[11] According to the gospel of thinness, my mother was supposed to hate herself, to hate the body she was in, and to work to reduce it, disappear it, discipline it in any way she could.

I think about her now when I look down at my own fat belly and see my double chin in photos. I was afraid of this happening for so long and it took me a long time to examine and confront that fear. And it is literal fear, I believe. "Fatphobia" is one of the most appropriately named of the prejudices, because while it functions in society in ways that are similar to other bigotries, it also contains an actual, real fear at the heart of it. Fatphobia evokes, for the thin person, a demonstration (however erroneously) of the morality and flexibility of bodies. Like the bodies of people with disabilities invoke an existential dread of the abled—a reminder that if we live long enough, we will all become disabled—the thin person views the fat person in the same way. The thin person is afraid that their carefully exercised control and their sacrifice is all for naught—that they are not, actually, the ultimate arbiters of their health.

Fat has long been shorthand for ill health—often erroneously so. Fat people are believed to be literally killing ourselves with overeating in the most uncharitable versions of fatphobia I've encountered. Over the years, work from fat activists and improved work on what fat *actually* means have caused a notable shift in the argument. In the 1990s, the questions were always of weight control, weight loss, but in the last two decades, the culture has shifted significantly toward "wellness culture." It's diet culture rebranded, all about "getting healthy" and "staying fit"—which are all code for thin. This shift masks the fatphobia that's still widely present in American culture—outright condemnation of fatness has been replaced by "concern" for our health. But very often, this concern simply covers up for what is actually fear and disgust that fat people dare have bodies and exist in public.

This moralization of health comes from the fact that health is largely invisible. We live and exist in these forms that we only really started learning about deeply and intimately within the last couple centuries. Until the 1800s, we didn't know that tiny little invisible things called bacteria and viruses—more colloquially "germs"— were the cause of disease. Prior to that, the dominant theory was that there was "bad air" that floated around and made people sick (known as the miasma theory of disease). But once we figured out that germs existed and were the real cause of illness, medical science was able to leap forward in its work, though it wasn't always linear. It took a lot of work and a lot of pushing to get doctors to adopt handwashing protocols that are now simple everyday procedure (or, at least, we hope they are) for literally everyone. And it took a long time before doctors actually understood things that we now know to be true, like the fact that babies can feel pain (up until the 1980s, it was common to operate on infants without anesthesia because of a mistaken belief that babies didn't actually process pain).

What we think we know about our bodies might change tomorrow with a new discovery or a new pandemic. In daily life, we accept some level of risk—if we didn't, we wouldn't be such a car reliant culture—but the invisibility of health defies all of our ability to control things. This is part and parcel of why fat bodies are such a challenge to "health" culture. For centuries now, fat bodies have been symbols of unhealthiness, of an inability to control one's health. It is a mechanism for blaming the individual for a society-wide fear of the unknown.

Aubrey Gordon, New York Times Bestselling author and cohost of the podcast Maintenance Phase, calls this particular fear "healthism." She writes,

> The cultural mandate for people to lose weight isn't about health—it's about power and privilege. The logic goes like this: fat people have failed to effectively perform health for the thin people around us. Thin people have succeeded where those fat people have failed, their perceived health evident in their thinness. . . . Fat people are positioned as inept and irresponsible keepers of our own bodies, and we must be corrected and saved by the thin experts around us.[12]

Gordon's use of the word "saved" there is not accidental. Fatness is condemned in part to allow thin people to view themselves as the saviors, the do-gooders of Health and Wellness. But the reality of what actually happens feels much less like salvation and more like damnation. In the name of serving this invisible god of health, fat people are encouraged to make their bodies smaller, to take up less space, to have no special accommodations or needs. We are punished for daring to exist in a body that demands accounting for, that takes up space.

This fear of losing control over one's body is extremely harmful. For fat people, it means discrimination in employment, isolation socially, and potentially severe detrimental health effects. And when thin people are assumed to be healthy, it can come as a shock when they acquire an illness or have trouble normally attributed to fat people (like cardiac issues). What's more is that dieting culture—a culture that convinces you to assuage your fear of your own body by dieting it away—can lead to severe harm to one's overall health.

Consistently yo-yo dieting, constant fluctuations in weight, can lead to cardiac problems later in life because it weakens the heart muscle.

But none of that reality matters in a culture that fears and hates fat people so much that being *kind* to one is considered brave. I'd like to close here with two contrasting pieces of culture: 2022's *The Whale* and the general existence of Lizzo.

I've always been a fan of Brendan Fraser. *George of the Jungle* was one of my favorite movies as a kid, and boy, do not get me started on *The Mummy*, a masterpiece of adventure cinema. Fraser disappeared from the Hollywood scene in the 2000s, in large part a reaction to his being sexually assaulted by the head of the Hollywood Foreign Press Association, the group most well-known for voting for the Golden Globes. So by 2020, after this history was revealed in 2018 in a profile in *GQ* ahead of Fraser's return to acting, pop culture was chomping at the bit for a comeback story. And in 2022, Fraser got it. He made an Oscar-winning turn as the main character of a new Darren Aronofsky film called *The Whale*. In the movie, Fraser plays a depressed, gay, and dying 600-pound man who is so ashamed of his own body that he has pushed everyone and everything away. It's supposed to be a poignant story about a depressed father (Charlie) figuring out how to reunite with his teenage daughter (Ellie).

But the movie is, as writer Lindy West calls it, aggressively violent toward fat people. West wrote a perfectly respectable, extremely well-argued review of *The Whale* for the *Guardian*, but here, I am going to quote her "Butt News" newsletter, where she published something a bit more candid:

> Ellie asks Charlie why he gained all that weight and he said, "Someone close to me passed away and it had an effect on me." Okay, sure, maybe. Is it that simple? Do you know what I mean when I say that fat people aren't allowed to have nuanced relationships with our own bodies? You have to either be like "yes I am powerless before ham and I deserve punishment" or "no I'm actually

perfectly healthy and happy and I only eat beautiful salads." Pure penance or pure defiance. But our lives are just as complex as anyone else's! Fat people should be able to say "yeah I have weird shit about food" or "yes my body hurts" without validating trolls' meanest fictions about us! JUST LEAVE US ALONE UNLESS WE ASK.[13]

In the name of concern, of compassion, fat bodies get reduced to simplicity. When we are not receiving hatred, we are receiving pity. We are, either way, not allowed to be human, and we must be punished. Part of the truly disgusting discourse around *The Whale* was its self-congratulatory promotion as something showing *compassion* to fat people, of showing what our lives are really like. Apparently, our lives are really self-hating heart attacks waiting to happen. We are not allowed to be happy and fat because if we are, then we are betraying everything we are supposed to be. We must engage in this fear-dance!

Speaking of happy fat people: Lizzo. Lizzo is a Black singer and rapper who grew up in Houston, TX, and moved to Minneapolis, MN, in her twenties to start her music career. She broke into the mainstream in 2018 with the song "Truth Hurts," which became the song of the summer that year, even though it was actually a couple years old. This revival of Truth Hurts boosted her 2019 album into an official hit, and in 2022, she became the first Black woman in nearly thirty years to win a Grammy for Record of the Year (since Whitney Houston won for "I Will Always Love You.").

Lizzo is also a big girl and happy about it. She works hard to boost the careers of other fat Black women and embraces her body in a way that is honestly truly inspiring as she just does not care (or let it show if she does care) about any negativity she receives. She also talks openly about her position as a fat person. In a TikTok video that conveniently was posted while I was writing this chapter, Lizzo addressed the way thin people view her as a fat person, especially as a fat person who works out and is vegan: "I think a lot of people see a fat person that way and immediately just assume everything they're doing is just to be thin. I'm not trying to be thin. I don't ever want to be thin. . . . My body is going to change. Everyone's bodies change. That's life. That's what human existence is. You a baby, and then your body continues to change forever until it stop."[14]

The simple acceptance that we are who we are, we exist in the bodies we have, and yes, our bodies exist in time and space and are subject to the laws of physics, including entropy. Fat people, thin people, healthy or not: we all have to deal with the fact that we have bodies, so we should probably stop being so afraid of them.

4 | THE DISABLED BODY

In 1881, it was illegal to be ugly in public in Chicago. Like many other cities around the United States, Chicago passed laws that criminalized the public appearance of people who were "diseased, maimed, mutilated, or in any way deformed, so as to be an unsightly or disgusting object."[1] These "ugly laws" were the precursor to the popular eugenics movement of the early twentieth century and were used to prevent people with visible disability, or who were unhoused, impoverished, or otherwise disadvantaged, from participating in public life. The particular phrasing of the Chicago law is striking as it deliberately treats people affected by the law as objects, no longer persons. It makes explicit the purpose of the laws—when introduced in San Francisco, the ostensible purpose was to prevent begging on the street, but in Chicago it morphed into a direct attack on the existence of disability in public.

The Eugenics Archive, a project funded by the government of Canada in the province of Alberta, documents the eugenics movement of the early twentieth century and behind, tracing the rise of the movement designed to improve human stock, as though we are all for sale in a market. It catalogs the stories of people who survived eugenics laws and is one of the best databases we have tracing the impact of eugenicist ableism throughout North America. Eugenics, broadly, was a popular movement among the elite in America dedicated to solving the "problems" of disability, poverty, and other maladies by simply breeding them out of existence. If we prevented disabled people, criminals (often considered an overlapping group), and the "mentally deficient" from reproducing, we could, evolutionarily, get rid of disability within generations.

The impulse from this was largely class-centric, and of course ableist. But it was also, I contend, based in fear of the body. For that, I need to go back to the 1990s to my family's story.

Despite my parents marrying young, at twenty-two years old in their senior year of college, they waited to have children until many of their loans were paid off and their careers in teaching had been established. So about nine years into their marriage, they decided to start. My mom was around thirty or thirty-one, and it was the early 1980s. Right before the new year at the tail end of 1982, she went into labor with my oldest brother. Labor didn't go well, and she had to have an emergency C-section, at which point the doctors immediately absconded with her newborn son and my parents learned the news: he had Down syndrome.

Matt spent the first few weeks of his life in the neonatal intensive care unit, as the doctors were watching for cardiac complications common in Down syndrome infants. My parents discussed how to prepare for this surprise and they brought him home when he was healthy enough to go. He was their kid, and they were going to raise him. It took my extended family a little bit to get used to the idea—my dad told me once that my grandpa had asked him when he was going to grow out of his condition.

Just a couple years before my brother was born, President Jimmy Carter had organized a Presidential commission on mental health, resulting in the Mental Health Systems Act of 1973, which provided financing to deinstitutionalize people with disabilities and worked to mainstream them into society. This was in large part due to a parents' movement in the 1940s and 1950s (which I mentioned in chapter 2) that insisted children born with developmental and intellectual disabilities could stay home instead of being whisked off to institutions, where they were segregated from society and often suffered from cruel abuses. So by the time Matt was born into a South Dakota hospital on New Year's Eve, 1982, it was considered normal practice for my parents to take him home and raise him with his own family.

Growing up with an older brother who has Down syndrome changed how I perceived ability from an early age. I was fiercely defensive of my brother, which showed up most readily in me lecturing my classmates that "retarded" was inappropriate and a slur and you need to stop saying that around me right now. I may have gotten into a few fights over it, including a complaint about a teacher who used the term in class and tried to wave it off by claiming to have a cousin who was fine with it. I also got to see the mainstreaming movement in action, as "special education" programs were incorporated into schools across South Dakota and students with intellectual or developmental disabilities were in school with abled classmates for the first time. I knew what an IEP—individualized education plan—was from a young age as my parents would have meetings with the schools about my brother's IEP while I waited in the lobby of the school district administration building.

Had my brother been born a century earlier, he likely would not have survived birth. But if by some miracle he was able to make it, he would've been subject to the Ugly Laws, which prevented people who looked like him from existing in public, largely because they were deemed "unsightly." But disability was also criminalized because an able-bodied public positioned disability, mental illness, and other chronic issues as criminalities in and of themselves.

The cause and effect were, of course, reversed: mental illness and disability did not *cause* criminality, but rejection from society as a result of those conditions forced people with disabilities to the margins where survival often required less than legal means. But with the eugenics movement sweeping the elite, the coupling of criminality with the disabled body made it possible to push disability out of sight altogether.

In contrast to Darwinism or Natural Selection, which argued that those fittest to survive would carry on their genes in nature, eugenics was based on a related but different theory called "degeneracy." This kind of deterministic theory argued that criminality, poor behavior, and poverty were comorbid with mental illness and disability—that is, living an immoral lifestyle is what led to the disability. The "impurity" of the body was a natural consequence of the impurity of the soul. "Protecting children" was also a justification: in 1916, a disabled woman in Portland, Oregon, was forced out of town because of these so-called Ugly Laws—she was "too terrible a sight for children to see."[2] It is impossible to separate the pervasive fear of physical defect, of disabled bodies, from the eugenics movement, which intellectualized that fear and positioned itself as the arbiter of bodily perfection.

In the United States, the eugenics movement and research into eugenics as a potential good for society were funded through work from the Carnegies, the Rockefellers, and other industry tycoons of the day. By the 1920s, it was extremely popular among the elite white class in America to embrace eugenics and support its aims. For these people, it was framed by and large as a movement for the betterment of society—by getting rid of degenerate sinners who were dirtying the gene pool, we could self-select for a society composed only of great minds built for further industrialization and America's status as a nation of great minds and great people.

This meant, in practice, laws that prevented people deemed "unfit" by the State from movement in public spaces and from the right to marry as well as laws that sanctioned compulsory sterilization. In the 1920s, a young woman named Carrie Buck was deemed feeble-minded (an actual diagnosis at that time) by her adopted family and sent to an institution for people thought to be unfit. Thanks to Virginia law at the time, Buck was subject to compulsory sterilization without her consent. And because Virginia wanted to shore up its laws on the issue, a case was brought on Buck's behalf that went all the way to the Supreme Court. In an 8–1 decision in 1927, the court sided with Virginia in saying that Buck's civil rights were not, in fact, violated when a surgeon working on behalf of the State cut her open and removed both her fallopian tubes at eighteen years old. Justice Holmes, writing in the majority opinion issued by the court, affirmed that the "welfare of society may be promoted . . . by the sterilization of mental defectives."[3] Holmes goes on to argue that, like men sacrificing their lives for the good of the nation in war:

> It would be strange if [the State] could not call upon those who already sap the strength of the State for these lesser sacrifices, often not felt to be such by those concerned, in order to prevent our being swamped with incompetence. It is better for the world, if instead of waiting to execute degenerate offspring for crime, or to let them starve for their imbecility, society can prevent those who are manifestly unfit from continuing their kind.[4]

Buck v. Bell has still not been overturned.

It was this compulsory sterilization that interested those in the burgeoning Nazi Party in Germany the most. As the American eugenics movement was developing, creating philosophical arguments for why degenerates need to be prevented from procreating and kept from a "sane" society, its scientists were also sending their information over to Germany, where the nascent authoritarianism and ethnic cleansing movement were building steam. Hitler himself admired the way in which Americans had so quickly destroyed the "degenerates" in our midst—a group that just so happened to neatly align with marginalized races and genders as well.

In the 1930s, as part of a set of laws put forward that dehumanized both Jewish people and populations believed to be corrupted by Jewish influence and corruptions of Volkish ideology (LGBT people in particular, but also BIPOC and political radicals), the Nazi party disallowed "race-mixing" or intermarriage between Jews and people of other faiths. Their models in doing so were wholly American—they looked extensively to American miscegenation laws in order to start their work on pushing Jewish people to the margins. Such laws relied on models of race and disability that shared the same eugenicist root: the non-normative bodies of specific groups meant the state had a compelling interest in preventing their proliferation, and they absolutely had an interest in preventing their mixing with the white, able-bodied upper class that was going to carry on the best of the human race.

Disgust at non-normative disabled bodies and racism aimed at black bodies that were marked as obviously different was a driving force behind the eugenics movement, which pushed disabled individuals into institutions, brought the brutality of the State down upon Black bodies, and destroyed lives in the interest of preserving a genetic purity and preventing "degeneracy." For one nineteenth-century scientist, "criminal" had physical traits that could be identified and bred out of society—large and protruding cheek bones, for example, and a thick strong jaw—thus tamping down criminality. "Darker skin" was, of course, a given.[5] In this era, Dwayne "The Rock" Johnson would've been viewed as having criminality built into his genetics, what with his symmetrical face and high cheekbones.

The disabled body presented a quandary for the able-bodied upper class at the turn of the twentieth century, and it would be decades still before disabled people would win the right not to be treated as second-class citizens on the basis of their non-normative bodies. That's not to say everything is peachy-keen now. The same motivation that drove eugenicists of the early twentieth century now drives much of the twenty-first-century conservative movement, especially as regards disabled bodies. President Trump made several remarks during his 2016 campaign about disabled journalists, even at one point doing a gross imitation of a journalist's disability. But his ableism showed up in far more ways than just that.

In speaking to a nearly all-white crowd in Bemidji, MN, at a campaign rally in September 2020, Trump appeared to praise the breeding stock of white Minnesotans: "You have good genes. A lot of it is about the genes, isn't it, don't you believe? The racehorse theory. You think we're so different? You have good genes in Minnesota."[6] He went on to say "Every family in Minnesota needs to know about sleepy Joe Biden's extreme plan to flood your state with an influx of refugees from Somalia, from other places all over the planet."[7] Trump's obsession with good genes, as Brandon Tensley notes at CNN, has been lifelong, and its seamless integration into the conservative movement echoes the eugenicist movement of a century before, where the goal is producing "good genes" for the future of the human race.

This is a common refrain from conservatives nowadays, especially conservative Christians. Disability is not viewed merely as a different way of having a bodymind but an objectionable suffering that must be endured for any caregiver. By the same coin, disabled people are objectified in a different way but still "valued" for what they may teach able-bodied people, not for being people in their own right. And it still leads to eugenicist policies that deny disabled people agency, relationship, and independence.

The megachurch helmed by John Piper here in the Twin Cities— the very same one that produced the "empathy is a sin" thinking discussed in chapter 1—has had a lot of not great things to say on disability. Throughout the work on disability produced by Desiring God, the website for John Piper's ministry, one question is returned to again and again: Will the disabled person go to heaven? Will God "save" them? This question obsesses them.

In one article, a father writes, "I know well the joys and challenges of loving a child who ages in years but continues to function at a very limited cognitive level. Oh how our hearts long for him to know and treasure Christ and be restored from his broken body living in a fallen world."[8] In another, a different father likewise wonders, "Is my only hope and comfort that someday he'll be covered by the grace of God as he enters his rest? Am I just hanging on until he (or I) dies and enters this rest?"[9] Repeatedly, adult people with intellectual or developmental disabilities are compared to and treated as infants, where an abled infant and a disabled adult are considered the same before God because the only thing that matters is the ability of their minds and soul to comprehend the concept of sin. The first father mentioned above is writing his piece as addressed to a friend whose fifteen-year-old disabled daughter died, and says

> Hannah was a beautiful young lady. She was fearfully and wonderfully created by Jesus and for Jesus (Psalm 139:14; Colossians 1:16). And now she is joyfully glorifying her God with a perfectly restored body, free from all the effects of living in a sinfully broken world. She is free from hindrances in her mind and heart as she unreservedly lives in the everlasting delight of her glorious God.[10]

Hannah has no bodymind of her own, no sovereignty, no personhood. Her disability is wiped from her in this afterlife that the author imagines. And her disability is the *result* of a broken, sinful world. Instead of associating disability with criminality as the eugenics movement did, the evangelical movement of a century later has decided disability is the result of the sinful, broken world we live in—and therefore, as the logical conclusion goes, a punishment for the world's sin.

The disabled body in evangelicalism is a teaching tool, a mechanism by which an able-bodied parent may learn to cope with suffering and pain, inscribing that pain upon her child's body as though his inability to be "normal" is a trial to be endured, not simply a variation on human life and a person in his own right with differing needs. A disabled child exists to teach the parent something about God, an autistic mind is an angelic innocent who lays bare our social niceties, and a physical ailment is simply a thing to overcome, to battle, to win. Just as the eugenicists of a century ago viewed disability as a sin of poor breeding, a harm to society, evangelicals now view disability is an infantile regression, a sign of a broken world, and a thing their child will eventually be *cleansed* of, as though erasing their disability can somehow still give them the same person they knew in life. The disabled body is evidence of corporate sin in flesh.

Such implications—that disability or mental illness meant criminality or sin—aren't just a thing of the past. Despite my own brother's obvious disability, I grew up in a family that was not great about invisible disabilities. When I was in middle school, my grades tanked. I was previously a top student, but for some reason, I just could not get it together. My folders, backpack, and locker were a disorganized mess. No matter how much I tried to color-code my work, I would forget notebooks at home, bring the wrong textbook to the wrong class, and lose track of homework squished somewhere between other papers either in my room or my locker or sometimes even just in the car.

Looking back, it's obvious I was struggling with undiagnosed ADHD. What had been in childhood an occasional distractibility and tendency to unconsciously hum (even when sitting in a quiet classroom) turned into a full-fledged inability to stay attuned to the world around me and to stay organized. People who know me now might be surprised to hear that because I am now a scrupulously organized person, with set places for everything I need, and a massive investment both in time and money in organizational systems (bullet journals, I wanted to love you, I really did). All of that is because of how awful middle school was for me.

There have been several comments from my family about that time when I was struggling. Most of them got lost to time but two in particular have stuck around: one was my brother telling me when we were in college that my parents had worried I was going to grow up to be a criminal because I obviously wasn't good at school. And then, over a decade later, my sister-in-law told me about a conversation she'd had with my father where he attributed my disorganization during that time to teenage rebellion—apparently I *wanted* to fail and was doing so to get back at him.

Apparently, not being able to concentrate and being disorganized in school meant I was both a rebellious teenager and headed for a future of crime. I realize now, of course, that this was old school "degeneracy" talk being filtered into judging me for struggling with ADHD—a neurodivergence that made it hard for me to cope in rigid, structured settings like school. The idea that we need to reject bodies and minds that are different from the norm in ways we as a society don't yet understand appears to be alive and well in the conservative family.

This tendency, to think in an erasing or curing way about disability, is rooted in fear of the body. Each of us who is currently "able-bodied" and "able-minded," should we live long enough, will eventually see ourselves become disabled, simply by the process of aging. As a kid, I had a lazy left eye—it would drift off on its own—so I wore glasses from preschool to around third grade, when the muscles in my eye strengthened enough to hold the eye in place properly. It wasn't until my late twenties when I began developing headaches looking at the computer screen, when my vision would blur in the morning and take longer and longer to clear, that I realized I needed to go back to the eye doctor and get checked. And, as suspected, that doctor gave me a prescription and put me back in glasses. My muscles had weakened with age, and my lazy eye had returned, just subtly enough that it was causing issues with my vision. My "disability" had returned.

But my disability is so understood and so common that I don't necessarily need accommodations. My last eye doctor handed me my prescriptions and told me it was fine for me to buy glasses online. I spent forty dollars on the pair I'm wearing as I type this. And no one discriminates against me for wearing glasses, for needing accommodation because this particular kind of personal medical device is so ubiquitous that it's not even seen as a disability, necessarily. It simply returned with age. My brother, similarly, had to get glasses for the first time in his life at thirty-eight.

But the disability that comes with age isn't always so easy. When I was in my twenties, my mother began having memory problems. She was always kind of forgetful, and we had family jokes about her pointing to a part of the room and saying "bring me that. . .that. . .thingie."

"Which thingie, Mom?" we'd say as we pointed to various objects, eventually landing at the one she wanted (usually a blanket or a remote controller). We'd laugh and tell her what the name was and she'd go "oh I know! I just couldn't think of it!"

This went on for years, until my dad took her in to the doctor because the problems were getting worse. We then got the diagnosis that she had actually been having mini-strokes for probably years and as a result had a form of dementia. What the doctors didn't uncover at that time was the cause—that wouldn't come until a couple years later, when she was weeks from dying. She had amyloidosis, a disorder where her body overproduces amyloid proteins, which is essentially like throwing a wrench into the gears of the machine that is a person's organs and nervous system.

The thing I was not prepared for—insofar as you can prepare for your mother to die when you're twenty-seven—was the dementia getting worse. I spent a lot of time sitting in her hospital room, reading books and doing work or watching TV with her. At one point, she told me very sincerely that the nurse said she was going to see a neurologist. I knew this because Dad and I were the main advocates for her care. But then she said something off kilter: "His name is Dr. Johnson. He helped me with my epilepsy when I was a kid."

It occurred to me that that would mean her neurologist was nearing ninety years old, but who knows, maybe he is still practicing. Until I brought it up to my dad, who gave me a worried look and explained that she was probably experiencing further dementia, forgetting that it was 2014, not 1960. The incident scared me. Seeing my mother lose track of what year it was, of where she was, was extremely scary—the "mind" part of her bodymind was disappearing, and I had to get to know this new person who was still my mother, but fading.

It's hard not to imagine that, if there is an afterlife, my mom is, in fact, herself in it. But that self would also include her glasses, her fatness, and her dislike of anything spicier than paprika. She would still fall asleep in front of the TV watching the same Bones episode for the fifth time. And she would still love cats and delight in seeing photos of kittens from the Humane Society. "Thingie" would still be part of her vocabulary. It is impossible for me to imagine my mom outside of her body or "restored" to a body different from the one I knew her to have throughout my life. But I can fully understand why it would seem comforting that those disabilities—those things that ravaged her mind well before her body gave in—would not follow her in death. But I also have to confront that if I let that fear dictate my theology, dictate how I view the world and other people, then I have to understand what the implications of that idea are for *all* disabilities.

Is the problem the disability or is it the inaccessible and ableist world that turns difference into disability? Is the way we approach disability built out of fear for what could happen to our own bodyminds, should accident, or age, or disease take parts of who we are from us?

Disability studies is an academic field that emerged out of disability community activism in the 1970s. In 1976, the Union of the Physically Impaired Against Segregation (UPIAS) in London put out a booklet of fundamental disability principles, and from those principles a discourse emerged that eventually became the field of disability studies. In that slim booklet, UPIAS declared:

> In our view, it is society which disables physically impaired people. Disability is something imposed on top of our impairments, by the way we are unnecessarily isolated and excluded from full participation in society. Disabled people are therefore an oppressed group

in society. It follows from this analysis that having low incomes, for example, is only one aspect of our oppression. It is a consequence of our isolation and segregation, in every area of life, such as education, work, mobility, housing, etc.[11]

This became known as the social model of disability. Essentially, disability would not necessarily exist in a world that is completely accessible. Rather than being forced to adapt to an inaccessible world as disabled people, the world instead should be changed so that accessibility and care is the norm. This fundamental principle lays the groundwork for a systemic justice mindset in disability—that it is systems of injustice that create oppression, not individual actors. This shift in thinking changed how disability advocacy worked, both over in the UK, where the group was, and in the United States, where disability activists were already working toward the implementation of non-discrimination laws to protect people with disabilities. The disability rights movement, as it was known at the time, prioritized non-discrimination and recognition of accessibility as a primary concern. What started as a parents group eventually became a group centering the voices and bodies of those most affected by a discriminatory society.

Nancy Eiesland, a scholar in disability studies and Christian theology, writes in the 1994 book *The Disabled God* that Christian theology tends to go one of two ways: "either divinely blessed or damned."[12] She goes on to say that "the obstacles that confront us in our daily lives are held in place by the images, ideas, and emotional responses of an able-bodied society."[13] Much of how disabled people interact with the world, both in religion and in the political sphere, is viewed through the lens of able-bodied storytellers whose dominant narrative demands a consideration of the person while ignoring the body they live in.

Disabilities are not things to be cleansed, or erased, or suffered through. They simply are. We can look, quite simply, to the disability justice movement to understand how people with disabilities *should* be treated in our culture and to work against how they have been and are still treated.

Sins Invalid, a BIPOC-led and founded disability justice organization, has articulated principles of disability justice that unapologetically reframe disability into an issue of justice that respects the bodyminds of disabled people beyond merely "accommodation" or "accessibility," which is what disability issues are so often reduced to. In 2023, I began working for a disability justice organization that embraces the Sins Invalid principles of disability justice, and as an able-bodied person who had long been on the edges of the disability movement, I found myself checking my own ideas about myself against the principles of disability justice, which can be summed up in three ideas: (1) Justice means solidarity across movements and across types of oppression, and we do not live single-issue lives, (2) each of us is whole people outside of what we may or may not produce in a capitalist enterprise, and (3) we are interdependent, relying upon the collective for our shared liberation.[14]

The anti-capitalist principle is a defining one for disability justice, for reframing how we change our thinking in order to truly change how we think about bodies. Most Americans have been trained since birth to value people based on what they can contribute—their productivity in a capitalist system. This is because American society is deeply classist at its heart—we believe that a person's worth is based in what they can produce, and the best stories are meritorious men (mostly men) overcoming their circumstances in order to make themselves a success. As a result, most of our presentations of disability in popular culture and in the news are people "overcoming" their disability, or moving "beyond" it in order to be a successful, productive member of society anyway.

But true disability justice calls upon us to rethink all of that. Some people will never be able to contribute in a capitalist system. They will never hold down a job or pay taxes out of a paycheck. But they still have immense value because human beings and human bodies are inherently valuable, as they are. A miracle, for a wheelchair user, is not that they may walk again, but flat sidewalks, integrated ramps, and wider doorways. My brother will not be cured of his disability. He will be exactly who he is because his bodymind is who he is, regardless of how much he takes or gives to this capitalist hellscape in which we live.

Similarly, American culture must reimagine its conceptions of sin and criminality. For far too long, "the flesh," the "body" have been symbolic images of the sin that afflicts and destroys, making easy the leap from sin to disability. Eiesland offers a corrective in that theology must imagine the collective, which she calls "holding our bodies together"[15]: "Instead of flagellating ourselves or aspiring to well-behaved 'perfect' bodies, we savor the jumbled pleasure-pain that is our bodies."[16] This is the reimagining of respect for our own bodies and for the bodies of others *as they are in the here and now* and not indulging the ultimately ableist vision that we are "restored" in heaven. As many disabled theologians have pointed out: the resurrected Christ still had his scars.

At the end of the day, fear of the body creates opportunity for some of the most vicious of bigotries. Fear of difference in public led to the criminalization of the disabled, which led to horrific consequences as abled upper-class white people decided they could choose how other people's bodies should be treated. And it is a fight we are still having. Immigrants to the United States are still being forcibly sterilized at detention centers because the fear of "foreign bodies" still pervades American politics. The fear that bodies existing in physical space are actually intensely consequential, and more important than hard work or talent, is a major blow to the conception of American meritocracy than most of America wants to admit.

5 | THE RACIALIZED BODY

I went to a small Christian college that was mostly white. I was in a strange point in my life where I did not want to associate myself with either political party and thought I could somehow rise above politics, which is an extremely naive position for a person to take. My privilege showed—during one advanced composition course that I was taking over the summer, we read an essay from a Black professor about how, despite her achievements, despite her position of relative power, she was still subject to racist taunts and reminded of her position in a racist society.

I did not understand the essay. At some point, I turned the discussion around to what labels are acceptable—African American or Black, and put the one Black student, William, in the class on the spot by asking him, quite bluntly, what he prefers. I'm amazed he put up with me for all those years, and we've remained friendly in the nearly twenty years since that incident. But then, he had learned very quickly at our college that casual and overt racism were just going to be part of his experience.

In our freshman year, he was living in the boys' dorm on campus. It's a small college—maybe 1500 students, and there are two freshman dorms: one for boys and one for girls. As was typical of dorms during that time period, everyone had a white board with dry erase markers on their door so that people could leave a message if they stopped by or needed to borrow something. I imagine in today's age of cell phones and ubiquitous unlimited texting, such white boards are no longer necessary. But in those days, those white boards were part and parcel of communication in the dorms.

One day, early on in that year, a fellow student took a permanent marker and drew a large banana across William's white board.

As a white student who was on campus at the same time, I remember the story flitting through campus, with many of the (nearly all-white) staff and faculty expressing concern that this happened. A committee for equality was formed. And then there was nothing. I don't remember anything further being done. William was brought into discussion with leadership about how to make campus better for students of color, but if anything functionally changed, I didn't see it.

This was no surprise to me. Just two years prior to this event there was a huge furor in the same town—where William and I had both gone to high school—when several white students started attacking Somali and Ethiopian students around the city. These students from the horn of Africa were placed in South Dakota as refugees from war, uprooted from their homes by violence and then shoved into life in mostly white, mostly conservative South Dakota—a South Dakota that, despite being closer to Canada than any other international border, had a government that frequently expressed "concern" over the "immigrant crisis."

White students in the town absorbed their parents' racism and directed it at the students with whom they shared classes. One day during lunch at my school, a bunch of white students and Somali students ended up in a brawl in the hallway outside the glass-walled principal's office—a foolish place to have a fight, if you ask me. A few days later, the news reported that an Ethiopian family whose children attended one of the other high schools in town had woken up to swastikas spray-painted on their fence.

The school board had meetings, community members were outraged, jokes about "Rough Rider Racism" were made—our school mascot was a rough rider, named after Teddy Roosevelt's posse. But the only tangible change I ever saw was the appearance of bumper stickers around town reading "Eracism"—which was meant to be Erase Racism, but to me just looked like "racism you do online." It was a solution put forward by white people who had no clear idea of what the impact of racism truly is, and for whom the concept of prejudice would always be an abstraction. No syllabi changed. No discussions were had with students as a whole. Meetings were held, to be sure, but nothing changed. White people would never feel the impact of fear and hatred deep in their body, and therefore would never be able to adequately address the problem.

There's a line from Ta-Nehisi Coates's book *Between the World and Me* that comes back around to me almost every time yet another black man's life is snuffed out at the hands of state authority. Rushed to publication in 2015 following yet another "reckoning" after the murder of yet another black man, this slim volume is a letter to Coates's son, grappling with the author's relationship to blackness and explaining the racism of the world and the nature of white supremacy to a child who does not yet grasp that humans can enact great evil. Early on in the book—literally ten pages in—Coates writes:

> But all our phrasing—race relations, racial chasm, racial justice, racial profiling, white privilege, even white supremacy—serves to obscure that racism is a visceral experience, that it dislodges brains, blocks airways, rips muscle, extracts organs, cracks bones, breaks teeth. You must never look away from this. You must always remember that the sociology, the history, the economics, the graphs, the charts, the regressions all land, with great violence, upon the body.[1]

The Black body is the battleground of politics—it is the desire to control such bodies that split our nation in two once before and has guided political policy throughout my lifetime. The politicians have found ways to cover such animus—Lee Atwater most famously suggesting using euphemisms for economic anxiety instead of racist slurs: "So you say stuff like, uh, forced busing, states' rights, and all that stuff, and you're getting so abstract. Now, you're talking about cutting taxes, and all these things you're talking about are totally economic things and a byproduct of them is, blacks get hurt worse than whites . . ."[2] But the racist idea remains, through the debate about what to do with police brutality to student loan forgiveness to universal health care.

During my college years, as I turned much more to evangelicalism but also was becoming disillusioned with conservative politics, I registered as an independent (my home state has closed primaries, which means you have to register with a political party) and declared myself to be apolitical. I still largely had conservative views, but I decided that it was more important that I not get involved, not pay close attention, and instead only concentrate on bringing forth G-d's Kingdom, which I felt could be done sans political action for a brief period of time. As a white person in red-state South Dakota in the mid-2000s, my ability to do this was shaped by the fact that I viewed myself as a default in politics—enough people who looked like me and thought like me were already in politics that I didn't feel a need to involve myself. I could sit back on my haunches and let other people deal, because by and large, what laws did or did not pass did not materially affect me. This centrist phase allowed me to treat the political sphere as a game I could opt out of, a world of sports teams with the presidency as the championship game.

Years later, I realize just how naive I was as a person with a uterus. During that time period, my home state, South Dakota, was trying extremely hard to ban abortion by popular vote. In 2006 and 2008, South Dakota put the question of banning abortion on the ballot, and both times, it narrowly failed. The goal of the move was to create a law that would result in a challenge that could be taken to the Supreme Court of the United States and eventually overturn the decision in *Roe v. Wade*. The fact that such a decision would greatly affect my own body did not enter into the equation for me, as I was a pro-life evangelical who believed that if I simply behaved properly, I would never have a need for an abortion and the people who did get abortions were simply not engaged in the proper behavior. I arrived at this conclusion largely because I believed in bodies as a thing to be controlled and subdued, not as a human part of oneself.

What eventually made it click for me involved the 2008 election. I graduated with my bachelor's in the spring of 2008, so my senior year and my first few months at graduate school contained a lot of discussion about the upcoming election. I was growing to like this new Obama guy. Thanks to a study abroad in Oxford, I'd been introduced to new ways of being and thinking that challenged the ones I'd been taught growing up. I had to think about things in new ways, and that was causing a shift in my politics, especially with regard to our obligation to the poor. So I was interested in him, and, more importantly, I did not like John McCain and I especially did not like Sarah Palin.

I was also growing disgusted with my fellow evangelicals freaking out about how Obama is the antichrist, when he was really just a neoliberal who didn't support the war in Iraq. It seemed clear to me that Republicans were reacting extremely hard to the fact that Obama is a Black man, and that was made even clearer when my (white) systematic theology professor walked into class one day, slammed his books down, and said, "You know what level of proof people have that Obama is the antichrist? My mailbox number here at the college is 666. That makes me the devil. That's the level of 'proof' these people are spouting." It struck me as obvious in that moment that something else was happening with this election that was unlike others I'd experienced in my lifetime.

As the election grew closer, the unhinged Republican attacks on Obama grew worse. I was visiting my brother down in Texas when the news broke that Obama attended a church with a pastor who occasionally preached sermons about America's racist past. My brother and I—both theology nerds at the time—listened and thought "that doesn't seem out of line for a progressive theology."[3] "God damn America!" is inflammatory, sure, but only when you divorce it from context—the sermon was about how the American government has consistently betrayed minority races, and anyone who is not a white man, and then turns around and expects the same people it is persecuting to be patriotic:

> When it came to treating her citizens of African descent fairly, America failed. She put them in chains, the government put them on slave quarters, put them on auction blocks, put them in cotton field [sic], put them in inferior schools, put them in substandard housing, put them in scientific experiments, put them in the lowest paying jobs, put them outside the equal protection of the law, kept them out of their racist bastions of higher education and locked them into positions of hopelessness and helplessness. The government gives them the drugs, builds bigger prisons, passes a three-strike law and then wants us to sing "God Bless America." No, no, no, not God Bless America. God damn America—that's in the Bible—for killing innocent people. God damn America, for treating our citizens as less than human. God damn America, as long as she tries to act like she is God, and she is supreme. The United States government has failed the vast majority of her citizens of African descent.[4]

Such a sentiment from a white man might've still been controversial but likely would not have created the firestorm it did. After all, just a few years earlier, the white evangelical church had spent a lot of money and a lot of time obsessing over racial reconciliation initiatives, and it made sense that a pastor would call attention to the sins of racism while preaching about how the American government is not G-d. But because the words came from the mouth of a Black man who did not hold back on his anger, the right wing was up in arms, arguing that Obama is the real racist because he clearly hates white people—conveniently sidestepping the truth of all the elements of racism and oppression cited in that paragraph.

The 2008 election taught this white South Dakotan that racism is alive and well and that there are a lot of people for whom navigating the world is invariably changed by how other people perceive their bodies.

The second thing that changed my mind was Bristol Palin. A couple months before the 2008 election, news broke that Sarah Palin's daughter Bristol, who was then 17 and unmarried, was pregnant. The campaign issued a statement that Bristol was engaged to the father of the baby and intended to get married and that, yes, they were choosing to keep the baby. Specifically, they said they were "proud of Bristol's decision to have her baby and even prouder to become grandparents."[5] The word "decision" stuck out to me. The entire way these Christian conservatives were talking about Bristol was to point out how pro-life the family is, but even they couldn't escape the language of choice when it came down to it. Ultimately, Bristol made the decision to keep her pregnancy—it was an assumed outcome, but it was still framed as a decision. And that was when I realized there was no way to discuss a pregnancy like that without talking about the decision to keep it. You literally cannot avoid the language of choice—it's so built in to how we discuss things like teen pregnancy that even when the daughter of the vice presidential nominee gets pregnant at seventeen, they still talk about it in the context of "making a decision."

These two moments combined knocked me out of my political centrism. I realized simultaneously that bodies matter and that it's impossible to talk about politics without acknowledging how they impact and fall upon differing bodies. How we move through the world physically and what social constructions we have built based on those physical realities *matters*.

But American culture loves to obscure that basic fact. We talk in numbers and budgets and deficits, not recognizing that each of those numbers represents someone's bodily experience changing intensely. This is why, I believe, the onset of the COVID-19 pandemic was so wildly polarizing: it made it extremely clear that we do not live in a vacuum, that we are not just independent brains floating through space but physical bodies that require care and protection, and sometimes that means working together to protect the bodies of others. But even then, as celebrities sang "Imagine" into their phones from the comfort of their bedrooms, delivery drivers and grocery workers were still being called in to work to provide food and needed medicine for the higher-class people working at home.

Policy, as a whole, is about whose bodies are deemed worthy of protection and whose aren't. The COVID-19 pandemic brought this to a forefront in a manner many had not seen before, but the Black Lives Matter movement also demonstrated those same principles. Whose bodies are worthy of protecting and those who are considered expendable by the State is the heart of political maneuvering and policy making. Who gets to be considered a legal body existing in public spaces is dictated by the history of white supremacy in America, of which White Anglo-Saxon Protestant culture has been a potent driver, baptizing the supremacist views with religious thought.

A saying comes up frequently in discussions of Republican ideology online, and it was left in a blog comment by an anonymous person using the screen name of Frank Wilhoit, a political scientist who died in 2010. The comment is thus: "Conservatism consists of exactly one proposition, to wit: There must be in-groups whom the law protects but does not bind, alongside out-groups whom the law binds but does not protect."[6] The principle is named Wilhoit's law but did not actually come from Wilhoit. Still, the statement is a solid distillation of what happens in the conception of the legal body within the political frame.

To explain: for certain classes of people, the law exists to protect their existence but does not require their cooperation or following of the law itself. For other classes—the out-groups, often determined through a white supremacist lens—the law exists to punish and exploit, but cannot be used to protect their rights or bodies. These out-groups must always behave perfectly in the face of authoritarian violence and oppression, or their right to exist without oppression will be revoked. The right to exist always comes on a tenuous basis, pushed out because of white supremacist fear and hatred of the body itself, particularly the Black body.

Martin Luther King Jr. himself saw as much in the aftermath of the *Brown v. Board of Education* decision that instructed schools to integrate "with all deliberate speed." Rather than speedy integration, however, what happened after was something of a stumbling saunter—schools resisted integration until troops had to be sent in to force it to happen. In his 1958 book, *Strive Toward Freedom*, King remarked:

> The forces of good will failed to come through. . . . If every church and synagogue had developed an action program; if every civic and social welfare organization, every labor union and educational institution, had worked out concrete plans for implementing their righteous resolutions; if the press, radio, and television had turned their powerful instruments in the direction of educating and elevating the people on the issue; if the president and Congress had taken a forthright stand; if these things had happened, federal troops might not have been forced to walk the corridors of Central High School.[7]

King's words are echoed in the current crisis of police brutality and the resurgence of lynching in the public sphere. As I was working on this chapter, in the first week of May in 2023, a former Marine strangled a Black man named Jordan Neely to death on the floor of a subway car in New York City in front of dozens of onlookers, some of whom leapt forward to aid in the killing. News media referred to the murder as a "vigilante killing." Numerous Christian conservative commentators hailed the ex-Marine as a hero. The victim was a Black unhoused man who apparently had been yelling about being thirsty and needing food and shelter. His bodily needs, his openness about his Black body being human just like the mostly white commuters who were his audience, stoked fear and discomfort—not because of anything he did but because of the nature of white supremacy that fears the Black body as an intrusive Other. The violence he was experiencing as an unhoused person who couldn't get proper food and shelter was subsumed into an excuse for his lynching, because he was allegedly "aggressive."[8]

One particular example of the Black body being cast as something other, something to be feared, is a common (mis)conception among law enforcement and first responders: excited delirium. Excited or agitated delirium is a surprisingly old diagnosis, stemming from the 1800s, to explain a series of symptoms that are described throughout numerous cases. According to a 2011 article in the *Western Journal of Emergency Medicine*, "all accounts [from the 1800s] describe almost the exact same sequence of events: delirium with agitation (fear, panic, shouting, violence and hyperactivity), sudden cessation of struggle, respiratory arrest and death. In the majority of cases unexpected strength and signs of hyperthermia are described as well."[9] The first time the diagnosis was actually used, however, was a century later, when it was described in cases of "cocaine-induced psychosis."[10]

This diagnosis was used to explain the deaths of twelve Black women in Miami who all died after consuming a small amount of cocaine. The researcher at the time commented that "For some reason the male of the species becomes psychotic and the female of the species dies in relation to sex," explaining that the fact that all the deaths were of Black women could be explained by further study: "We might find out that cocaine in combination with a certain (blood) type (more common in blacks) is lethal."[11] It was only after a fourteen-year-old Black girl was found dead with no cocaine in her system that the medical examiner revised his associate's diagnosis, noting that each of the women had actually been murdered. What had been attributed to "the crack epidemic" was in fact a serial killer targeting Black sex workers in the city. What's more is that according to contemporaneous newspaper reports, the women whose deaths were attributed to "excited delirium" were found by dumpsters, all naked from the waist down, in a clear pattern that should have been flagged by any detective worth his badge. Of course, it was not, because the medical examiner said it was not murder but some kind of cocaine-induced psychosis that killed these women. And the word of a white supremacist State overrode the reality of what the Black body was saying.

Thus, we know the roots of this diagnosis exist in anti-blackness, a deep fear of the Black body, and a desire to blame victims of murder for their fate, proposing that instead there is something about their bodies themselves that explains their deaths. Still, the man who had misdiagnosed excited delirium refused to accept that he was wrong, arguing that "I have trouble accepting that you can kill someone without a struggle when they're on cocaine . . . cocaine is a stimulant. And these girls were streetwise." He also further added that Black men may have some genetic factor that explains why they get diagnosed with "excited delirium" more than white people, despite most users of cocaine in that time period being white: "Seventy percent of people dying of coke-induced delirium are black males, even though most users are white. Why? It may be genetic."[12]

The "diagnosis" is not a real diagnosis—it is not reflected in the *Diagnostic and Statistical Manuals* or the International Classification of Diseases that doctors use to determine diagnosis of illnesses. It is not recognized by the American Medical Association, the American Psychiatric Association, or the World Health Organization. It seems to be used largely as an assessment by first responders in the field to explain deaths that happen in their custody. Such unqualified diagnosis in the field frequently—as studies have shown—leads law enforcement officials to use more force than necessary in order to subdue the "superhuman strength" induced by the condition of excited delirium. Indeed, this thinking showed up in the death of George Floyd, as Derek Chauvin's defense at trial attempted to claim that excited delirium was why three officers needed to kneel on the back of a man they already had cuffed. A version of it also shows up in the murder of Michael Brown, an eighteen-year-old Black man whose shooting death in Ferguson, MO, led to nationwide protests. Darren Wilson, the officer who shot Brown, claimed that he "felt like a five year old holding onto Hulk Hogan"[13] and described a scene in which Brown was apparently able to "charge" toward Wilson despite being shot five times in his torso.

The fake diagnosis of excited delirium is most frequently used to describe the actions of Black men who die in police custody, attributing a non-human strength and ability to them as a justification for the police force that was likely the actual cause of death. In a 2022 study released by the group Physicians for Human Rights, 56 percent of the deaths in custody attributed to "excited delirium" were men of color (Black and Latino).[14] As the PHR group puts it, unflinchingly:

> The diagnosis of "excited delirium" has come to rest on racist tropes of Black men and other people of color as having "superhuman strength" and being "impervious to pain," while pathologizing resistance to law enforcement, which may be an expected or unsurprising reaction of a scared or ill individual (or anyone who is being restrained in a position that inhibits breathing).[15]

This justification pathologizes resistance to State violence, positioning the body of the person resisting police brutality as the fault of the person brutalized and the police as disembodied robots who simply must react in prescribed ways for some vague "protection" of the community. The body of the Black man in particular is that which must obey the law perfectly, never react out of turn or say anything negative or move in any perceived wrong way but is not protected by that same law when offenses are done against him. Their bodies and movement through the world are pathologized and used to blame them for their own deaths at the hands of the State. Because of the white fear of the Black body, they are denied humanity.

Another way this disbelief about the humanity of the Black body enacts violence is in the medical establishment. In 2017, tennis star and one of the most decorated athletes in the world Serena Williams gave birth to her daughter, Olympia. She wrote poignantly in 2022 of how pregnancy and labor connected her to her body in new ways: "I was enjoying it, the work of labor. I was completely in the moment. I loved the cramps. I loved feeling my body trying to push the baby out. I wasn't on an epidural; to get through it, I was using my breath and all the techniques I'd learned from birth training (I had taken every birthing class that the hospital had to offer)."[16] The labor turned into an emergency C-section, which Williams embraced, relieved to have the decision made for her in the moment. And in the moments after, she was so delighted by her newborn that the pain of the sudden surgery did not seem to matter: "I spent the night in the hospital with my baby in the room. When I woke up, she was nestled in my arms. The rest of my body was paralyzed. I couldn't get out of bed because my legs were still numb, but it didn't matter. Alexis and I sat there, alone with our new baby. It was surreal to feel the presence of this third person in the room. Who was this new little creature?"[17]

But in her body, a danger lurked. She developed a cough that wouldn't go away and broke open her stitches. She knew she had a history of blood clots that could lead to a pulmonary embolism. She was having all the symptoms of clots and asked when she was going to have a heparin drip—a blood thinner designed to stop clots—but the nurse dismissed her. At some point, Williams had to demand that the nurse tell the doctor to start a drip, that she needed a CAT scan, and it needed to be with dye. The nurse responded: "I think all this medicine is making you talk crazy."

Serena Williams spent a week in the hospital and needed three additional surgeries to break up the clots that formed and to drain a hematoma at her C-section incision in her abdomen. Even as an international superstar athlete, she was dismissed and belittled, literally told she was crazy, when she knew exactly what her body needed and what her own medical history indicated was the right course. She wrote about the harrowing ordeal five years later for *Elle* magazine, noting:

> In the U.S., Black women are nearly three times more likely to die during or after childbirth than their white counterparts. Many of these deaths are considered by experts to be preventable. Being heard and appropriately treated was the difference between life or death for me; I know those statistics would be different if the medical establishment listened to every Black woman's experience.[18]

Williams's experience is emblematic of the treatment of the Black body in US medicine and in policy, especially the Black female body. In the early 1990s, Dorothy Roberts published the landmark work *Killing the Black Body*, which argues that the Black female reproductive space is at the heart of movements for justice, and control of the Black female body is a primary goal of a white supremacist system. She writes: "White childbearing is generally thought to be a beneficial activity: it brings personal joy and allows the nation to flourish. Black reproduction, on the other hand, is treated as a form of *degeneracy*."[19] Degeneracy should be a red flag for you, as we discussed in the previous chapter how degeneracy was a primary driver of eugenic theory in the early twentieth century. The IQ tests developed to demonstrate the principle of feeble-mindedness were also used to demonstrate that

"Blacks and recent immigrants from Southern and Eastern Europe were intellectually inferior to Americans of Anglo-Saxon or Scandinavian descent."[20] Never mind that these tests were given in English to people who did not speak the language.

Because of these embedded racist attitudes, the Black woman's relationship with the concept of reproductive freedom has always been fraught—she has never been able to operate with the assumption that her body is her choice. As Roberts writes: "The language of eugenics did more than legitimate birth control. It defined the purpose of birth control, shaping the meaning of reproductive freedom. Birth control became a means of controlling a population rather than a means of increasing women's reproductive autonomy."[21] The birth control movement that spelled freedom for white women trapped in abusive marriages was also a eugenicist movement that saw it as a way to control the reproduction of Black people deemed degenerate.

Roberts then traces the ways in which Black women's reproductive autonomy has etched its way through history on a track parallel to but entirely different from that of white women. In the 1960s and 1970s, when white women were struggling to access permanent birth control via sterilization and were being required to attend therapy in efforts to discourage the end of their fertility, Black, Indigenous, and other women of color were being forced into sterilization at high rates. While white women fought for the right to end their pregnancies via abortion under the specter of "Pro-life" violence in the early 1990s, Black mothers were subject to prosecution for delivering so called "crack babies," with hundreds of mothers separated from their children again due to so-called "degeneracy."

The roots of this treatment of the Black female body in America come back down to Protestant control and fear over bodies. Sabrina Strings, Chancellor Fellow and Associate Professor of Sociology at the University of California at Berkeley, writes that throughout the nineteenth century, white Christian women were centered as the moral conservators of the household and of American culture.[22] This included, Strings elucidates, upholding bodily standards that set them apart from the degenerate Black community. For Christian Anglo-Saxon women in that time period, who were the ones granted the purest form of whiteness (even Irish people at this time were not granted such access to supremacy), the less their bodies looked like the plumper, rounder bodies of the Africans enslaved by their husbands, the better. The white beauty ideal was seen not only as a form of white supremacy but a mechanism of moral superiority, a symbol of control over one's gluttonies and of being in a right moral center.[23] The closer a woman was to disappearing into nothingness, the closer she was to God. Black women, by their very nature and bodily inheritance, could not, therefore, have access to this moral superiority.

Strings writes that white women played a particularly important role in advancing this uniquely protestant racial agenda: "Middle-class women outnumbered men among converts in the Second Great Awakening, and they were also the main trumpeters of temperance and dedicated diet reform."[24] White women, who bore children and ran the home, saw their bodies as a site for moral reform and certitude, and their control over their diet and their weight were moral indicators of goodness, lest they develop love handles and appear like those of lesser races, like the Celts (Irish) or, worse, the enslaved Black Africans. The association of the slim white body with the Protestant ethic of racial superiority and restraint embedded the concepts of denial and self-sacrifice into the white conception of the body. Black women were and are denied agency because they could not be trusted to restrain themselves from immoral excess, as demonstrated by their bodies. This, the White Anglo-Saxon Protestants proclaimed, was true freedom.

But as Dorothy Roberts writes: "The abstract freedom to choose is of meager value without meaningful options from which to choose and the ability to effectuate one's choice."[25] In order to achieve *true* freedom, a person must not only be protected from government interference with their body, but also be supported by that government in what Roberts calls "an affirmative guarantee of personhood and autonomy." The white fear that drives the Black person's relationship with State violence must be driven out, disempowered, and defanged. The State does not merely have an obligation to do no harm but rather to affirmatively ensure that harms are remedied and people have equality of outcome as well as opportunity.

This means getting rid of the double standard that insists the law protects but does not bind white people and that it binds but does not protect Black people. It is not enough for police to merely stop brutalizing Black bodies, but instead if police are to exist at all, their role must be that of affirmative protection—providing access to services, de-emphasizing property crime, and providing substance abuse disorder treatment rather than exacting revenge for alleged crimes against property and the State. Reproductive *justice* then means decriminalization of poverty, governmental support for new mothers, equality in parental leave, and the ability to take such leave.

But this only works insofar as we are able to recognize that the fear of the Other's body and the divorce of the mind and body are *systemic* issues, cultural problems that must be shifted. To return to Martin Luther King Jr.'s *Strive Toward Freedom*, he recognizes quite easily that such a change is hard to effectuate. A Christian pastor, motivated by his Christian faith, King rebutted the popular belief of the day that the individual conversion to Christ would eventually result in an anti-racist society. King was working in a unique time, when white evangelicalism was moving away from previous apolitical fundamentalism to a much more politically active movement, in part to reclaim the Christian faith for a white, conservative movement. Scholar Curtis J. Evans sums up the shift:

> [White evangelical] conceptions of sin, social change, and personal ethics played a determinative role in their repudiation of the underlying social thought of legislation on behalf of black civil

rights. An individualistic approach to social change that placed paramount importance on personal regeneration (in an immediate conversion experience) was in conflict with the emphasis on social and systemic change advocated by Martin Luther King Jr. And those religious leaders who were generally sympathetic to civil rights for African Americans. Evangelicals lambasted liberal religious leaders for preaching a social gospel that neglected evangelism and personal regeneration.[26]

Thus, the mainline conservative position following a great advancement of civil rights for Black Americans, won through tireless protests and pushing back against violence, was to deny the collective nature of the struggle and instead focus on the individual body. Billy Graham, one of the most influential American preachers of the twentieth century, took the position that any change in race and politics must come from individual conversion to proper thinking rather than through legislative will.[27] How change would happen was left up to God—indeed, Graham seemed to take a fairly nihilist view that racism could not be resolved until Christ's return. In a ten-year retrospective on his evangelism for *The Christian Century*, one of the foremost publications of conservative evangelicalism, Graham wrote:

> I am more convinced than ever before that we must change men before we can change society. The international problems are only reflections of individual problems. Sin is sin, be it personal or social, and the word repent is inseparably bound up with evangelism. Social sins, after all, are merely a large-scale projection of individual sins and need to be repented of by the offending segment of society. But the task of the evangelist is not merely to reform but to stimulate conversion, for conversion puts man in a position where God can do for him, and through him, what man is incapable of doing for or by himself.[28]

But just three years later, Graham told the *New York Times* that he wished his "good personal friend" King would "put the brakes on just a little bit" in regard to the sit-ins, protests, and marches.[29] Though Graham could believe that "God has intervened more than once in history, and there is every reason to believe that he will intervene again,"[30] it seems God could not and would not intervene through the words and body of a Black preacher from Atlanta.

This attitude from Graham is reflected over and over in current cultural stands. In 2004, Russell Moore, then professor of Christian Theology and Ethics at the Southern Baptist Convention's premier seminary, Southern Baptist Theological Seminary, completely rewrote the history of white evangelicalism in the Jim Crow era:

> Jim Crow was not voted out of office. He was drowned, in a baptistery. Contemporary evangelicals, like most Americans, are prone to see the civil rights movement of the 1950s and 1960s as the triumph of secular Enlightenment egalitarianism. In fact, however, the civil rights movement drew on the imagery and vision of American revivalism. In so doing, the civil rights movement succeeded precisely because its proponents were able to shame the American conscience by appealing to a profoundly orthodox understanding of conversionism and churchmanship. With an underpinning of conservative evangelical concepts of soteriology and ecclesiology, American evangelicals were able to see that their sins against African-Americans in the oppressive Jim Crow power structures were about more than southern tradition. Instead, seg-regation and racial injustice were, at the gut level, a repudiation of the gospel of Jesus Christ.[31]

This seems kind of weird to say when the most famous evangelist of the time was telling Martin Luther King Jr. to put the brakes on and perhaps let moderation prevail. Despite Moore's misremembering and mis-stating of history in a way that wildly favored white evangelicals, nearly two decades later, the racism he saw happening within the Southern Baptist Convention ended up pushing him out entirely. His vocal stance against Trump was already causing trouble, but it seemed his concern for issues that recognize the integrity and reality of the body—sexual abuse within the SBC and racism he directly encountered as his fellow white people challenged his work on anti-racism within the church—led him to resign in 2022. It seems that even when a white evangelical attempts to make this work happen from within, in the littlest of steps, the cultural force of white fear will come down to silence his work.

We live in a country that was built on the economy of white Protestants and enslavers (often one and the same). America is, indeed, a Christian nation as that image of the body, the "soul" within it, and what the combination of the two means in the world has shaped and formed every bit of our culture—especially in regard to race. If the body does not matter, then, if we are all simply flesh in a colorblind society, then there is no need to confront the lived experience of those bodies that are not white. Better, then, to look always toward heaven, to imagine a soul unencumbered by the necessities of the flesh. Better to pretend that we are all equal at the foot of the Cross so that we need not examine how our own racism falls upon the Black body with a sickening thud.

6 | THE LGBT BODY

I had surgery to remove my breasts as the start of my medical gender transition in April of 2022, a couple months before my previous book, *In Transit*, was released. I'd never been sedated before, and I was all kinds of worried and anxious about it, but my desire to get the surgery over with outweighed all those worries. My friend picked me up just after 6 a.m., and everything after that is a blur. I remember sitting in my hospital bed as my surgeon drew rough lines of where she was going to cut. The anesthetist asked me about my dental history and I went "ah yes, my luxury bones," which thankfully he didn't hear or if he did, he ignored. Needles were put into the back of my hand, which made my pulse quicken enough that I had to take a few deep breaths to calm myself down.

Eventually I was wheeled into the operating room and asked to scoot over onto this little table. They took my arms and laid them out to my sides, extended onto little platforms and harnessed into place. I remember thinking "hah, like Jesus" before my world became nothingness. The next thing I remember is pulling an oxygen mask off my face and staring blearily at a nurse who was saying things I couldn't comprehend. As the world slid back into place, I looked down at my chest, covered in gauze and wrapped in an ace bandage, and thought to myself "wow, it actually happened."

The next two days were full of pain meds and me learning how to sleep sitting up. Apparently at some point, I turned to my friend who had accompanied me to surgery and said "I finally understand EDM."

I have no memory of this. The understanding has since been lost to my Percocet-induced high. I thought I would be scared to be in that drug-induced state—I have never once been drunk or high—but it turned out to be like wrapping a comfortable blanket around me, the perfect fuzziness that just wiped away any pain I was having. It was weird to have my friend tell me about the EDM (electronic dance music) comment months later, like finding out another version of yourself had been existing within your skin this whole time.

The following week, I emptied my own body fluid into a small cup to measure it before flushing it down a toilet, painstakingly sanitizing my hands before lightly pulling on the clear tubes that were running out of the sides of my torso in order to create suction in the drain bulbs. I spent my days on the couch, watching nonsense TV, talking on Twitter, and watching TikToks on my phone. Sometimes I played video games. Friends came by once every couple of days to drop off food and clean out the litter box. Despite the fact that I'd had major surgery, I didn't actually feel much pain. I was exhausted and I wasn't very hungry, but other than that, I wasn't hurting unless I did something dumb like trying to lay flat on the couch, which required the use of my abdominal muscles to get back up. I had never so closely encountered the reality of my body, examining it and listening for every bit of complaint or pain.

The weeks dragged on, and I eventually got to get rid of the compression band that was holding my chest together. The nipple bandages came off as the grafts healed up and the outer layer of scab sloughed off. My incisions went from an angry red to a lighter pink as new skin grew and scar tissue took over. When it's cold, the scars turn a darker purple color but nowadays stay mostly pink. They're obvious because I didn't do much scar care to try to make them fade—for me, that mattered less than the fact that my clothes finally fit like I wanted them to.

And within a month of surgery, I noticed a distinct change in my mental health. With a body that felt like home, that finally didn't surprise me when I looked in the mirror, my anxiety was dissipating like morning fog when the sun rises. For nearly a decade, I have been on some variation of mental health meds—a daily SSRI and an as-needed anti-anxiety med. I started out with the tougher stuff—Klonopin and then Xanax and then Ativan. In 2017, my doc switched me to hydroxyzine, which is an off-label use of a common antihistamine, because in trials the combination of meds had demonstrated efficacy in lowering anxiety symptoms. For five years, I'd needed that medication nearly every day, sometimes twice a day if the anxiety was really bad or if I'd triggered a panic attack with too many cups of coffee at work. I couldn't bear being in enclosed rooms; I required aisle seats on airplanes, and I had immense trouble attending movies without significant preparation. By 2022, I was certainly doing *better* than I had been when I was put on the medications, but I'd resolved myself at that point to a lifetime of needing to carry a bottle of anxiety medication with me wherever I went.

But a month after surgery, nearly all of that stopped. First I went a few days without the hydroxyzine. And then a week. And then two weeks. And eventually, I simply left the bottle at home in the medicine cabinet. I took it literally only when I needed it—on a flight to Los Angeles to promote my last book, and once after I was in a car accident. In the year following surgery, I needed my as-needed anti-anxiety meds all of four times.

Changing my body with medical transition cured me of an ailment that had been with me since I was a child. It was a miracle that connected me with my body in a way I never thought possible and helped me to recognize that what had been causing the anxiety for ages was actually gender dysphoria, morphed into a fear of being noticeably different, of not fitting in with my gendered role in society, and of not having a body that complied with what my conservative and wrathful God demanded of me. Suddenly a new idea was occurring: I was being made new, with the help of medical science, into something that aligned with who I was supposed to be and the body my brain had mapped out for me. Anxiety gone, I finally understood what transgender theorist Susan Stryker had meant when she said, "I want to lay claim to the dark power of my monstrous identity without using it as a weapon against others or being wounded by it myself. . . . Monsters, like angels, functioned as messengers and heralds of the extraordinary. They served to announce impending revelation, saying, in effect, 'Pay attention; something of profound importance is happening.'"[1]

That thing of importance is the transformation of the body, a person taking part in their own creation. The body is becoming, no longer in stasis, no longer a thing to be subdued and controlled as an enemy, but a gendered, sexual BE-ing. Transition grounds the body in the real world, takes it both for what it is and what it could be. There's a concept in philosophy from Martin Heidegger called "Geworfenheit," or "thrown-ness." For Heidegger, Geworfenheit is the moment when a being in the world realizes that it exists without one's consent or will—we are the ball recognizing that it has been thrown and it is headed toward the crack of a bat. Transition, then, is the response to Heidegger's Geworfenheit, a body, upon recognizing that it is in flight, changes its trajectory. My body is at once a site of profound self-revelation, and because it exists in physical, material space, it is also a site of profound change. And that idea butts right up against the way American culture views bodies altogether.

In 1991, conservative pastors John Piper and Wayne Grudem published the fundamental text of the complementarian evangelical movement: *Recovering Biblical Manhood and Womanhood*, a book of theology and exegesis examining the roles of men and women in the church and, importantly, in the home. This work was a response to the rise of evangelical feminism, in which evangelical women argued for equality in the church, the approval of women as pastors, and more ability to perform roles they felt God had called them to. Male leadership in the church responded by using the Bible to argue that female bodies were necessarily designed for particular roles and those roles were that of housewife, mother, and homemaker.

Much hay has been made about this narrow view of the bodies of men and women as represented in this movement throughout the 1980s and 1990s. I myself was raised in the evangelical purity culture of the early 2000s, and I chafed greatly at the idea that because I had a vagina at birth, that meant I was destined to be forever in a servant role—and destined to be heterosexual and married and having children. I was ambivalent about having kids from the get go, even though I learned quickly that voicing such ideas would result in a heavy rebuke, so I learned to fake it. When it came to imagining future children, however, I never got further than deciding his name would be Elijah (and that may have just been early trans identity showing through as I've always had great affection for that name).

It would seem, at first glance, that the work of asserting complementary roles for men and women based upon their bodies would be a sign of great concern for the body. After all, it is because of the body that a person falls into these specific roles. Indeed, the Council for Biblical Manhood and Womanhood argues that our roles from God are biologically based, that our bodies are formed by God to play out these roles. The Council formed in the 1980s when a group of mostly white, mostly male pastors determined that the problem with America is that men and women did not know their biblical roles. And they do not just argue from reproduction here—it is obvious, to them, that women are "designed" to give birth and so on—but rather they argue that our very *behavior* is determined by our bodies.

Bethel University (St. Paul) professor Gregg Johnson in fact argues that the hierarchal structure that men have formed in most cultures is evidence of the God-given behavioral ways to live:

> Anthropologists find similar kinds of universal sex-specific behaviors among human cultures. Of two hundred fifty cultures studied, males dominate in almost all. Males are almost always the rule makers, hunters, builders, fashioners of weapons, workers in metal, wood, or stone. Women are primary care givers and most involved in child rearing. Their activities center on maintenance and care of home and family. [. . .] The fact that these universals transcend divergent animal groups and cultures suggest that there must be more than a cultural basis for these sex differences. The data point to biological predeterminants of gender-related behavior. Indeed, as we survey the biology of mammals and humans in particular, we find sex-related differences in all of the organ systems, including the brain and nervous system.[2]

The prevalence of these supposed roles across cultures is evidence, Johnson argues, of a common thread of biologically determined roles that men and women must play. Individual bodies, individual conceptions of oneself, individual thoughts about gender do not matter as the body simply determines the category one must play in God's grand scheme. What feminists would and have argued is evidence of the pervasiveness of misogyny based on the biology that people assigned female tend to have, Johnson sees as evidence of God.

The gendered body, then, is simply another object to be controlled and subdued, understood not as its own unique thing but as evidence of a role God has handed to each and every person—and therefore a role that must be played. The body is subsumed into the role, individual characteristics and conceptions be damned. This was the world I grew up in—and it made me profoundly anxious. Because my role was imposed upon me by outside forces, by a God others believed in on my behalf, I developed severe anxiety about my own failure to live up to that role. I could sense the falsity of the concept deep into my bones but still felt I needed to lean into it to sacrifice my selfhood to God. The more I tried, however, the worse my anxiety got. My own body was rebelling, hard, against what my faith told me was necessary for living for Jesus.

I was quite literally and viscerally afraid of what listening to my body would mean, of what being at home in my own flesh would mean for my role in the world. I absorbed all these messages from my church about what dying to flesh and living in spirt would mean, about living in new life and new spirit, letting go of the old self. But I was experiencing a very different life within my flesh that no amount of spiritual will could overcome. My body—my trans-ness—demanded to be heard.

It is in LGBT issues—especially trans issues—that the American Protestant culture is most profoundly afraid of what the body means, and what it means if we truly inhabit them as though they are important and consequential parts of the life of the world. And the backlash against trans people in particular has only intensified in recent years as trans people have become more visible publicly and conservatives have become fearful about their hold in culture following the legalizations of same-sex marriage in *Obergefell v. Hodges* in 2015. The reactionary movement has turned its crosshairs right onto trans people—particularly trans youth—as emblems of everything they deem wrong with society.

Matt Walsh, one of the leaders of this anti-trans crusade, who provided fodder for the evangelical culture war with the release of his documentary, *What Is a Woman*, spoke in 2022 about the harms of medical transition. His words reflect a fear of having actual autonomous control over one's body. In this clip, he was speaking about a trans man named Gabriel Mac who wrote about his phalloplasty surgery for the *New Yorker*. To be clear, the "she" referred to here is actually a he, but I have preserved the misgendering as it makes his point (and his hatred of anyone he deems violating what he sees as the role of being a woman) clear:

> She doesn't look like a woman, certainly, but neither does she look like a man. She's in sort of a gender purgatory. What we find is we can reject the gift of our own physical selves by mutilating our bodies, but what we cannot do is create a new self. You know, when it comes to our selves, we only have the power to maintain or destroy, not to create. If you choose to destroy yourself, you'll be left with this, which is what all trans people who get surgeries are left with—you're left living in a prison of your own making, stuck like that forever.[3]

Here, I believe, Walsh hits the nail on the head in a way that exemplifies the overall fear of the trans body. For so much of white America in general, the idea that one might have the ability to *change* the body one was born with in such a significant way as to literally change gender is a terrifying prospect. Because of that fear of the body instilled throughout the history of white Protestant evangelicalism, incorporated into life as a principle of holiness, the idea that one could possibly be close enough in relationship with their body to co-create it is an impossible pipe dream. We are to fear the body, to fear the flesh and how it might cause us to sin, and we are to embrace the role our body determines for us. Shrugging off the idea that a body can't change and actively taking a hand in that creation is a great horror. The only acceptable change is to lose weight and become the ideal of a thin, cisgender person.

But Walsh is not alone in his thinking, and nor is the anti-trans movement solely a conservative one. Some atheist philosophers have chosen to engage in anti-trans thinking by using materialism—the idea that we are nothing but a body—to argue that sex assigned at birth is determinative of who we will become as a person. Kathleen Stock, who claims to be a materialist philosopher though her expertise is actually in philosophy of literature (which is not necessarily a materialist or idealist category), has dabbled in transgender philosophy for a time. But not believing in being a body inhabiting a soul, Stock has to rely instead on an argument from history—that a material body, once assigned to a category and once existing within a specified concept of biological sex, cannot thus be changed.

Stock's work represents a specific transphobia, a specific fear of the body that is housed in personal fear for one's own sense of self. Throughout Stock's book, *Material Girls*, it is deeply important that people are able to fit into two different clusters of human, male or female, as that is how the world is ordered. Repeatedly, she relies on the history of a person's assigned sex, the previous knowledge of a trans woman having had a penis, for example, as proof for the idea that a trans person's gender is illegitimate in any case. Unlike the evangelicals, who rely on a more coherent theology of "God created us this way and this is who we are when living godly lives," Stock must instead rely on the fear of "maleness" in order to create her argument. In arguing that sex—that is, the biological history of a trans person— is vital to how the world conducts itself, Stock argues that cisgender women will become afraid of speaking up against people who should not belong in restrooms:

> Since gender identity is not something anyone can see directly, and is supposedly potentially detached from behaviour, dress and physiognomy, practically speaking this means that any male at all can enter a space and claim, if challenged, that it aligns with his gender identity. . . . [F]emales are expected not to challenge but just to "carry on" with their own business. This obviously puts them at additional risk of assault.[4]

Throughout my reading of Stock's book, I kept wondering to myself when she was going to get to an argument about why trans people shouldn't be allowed to change their bodies, shouldn't be allowed to take control of themselves in such a way as to become a new person, a new material self. And again and again, I kept returning to her fear— her fear of a loss of special class somehow encroached by allowing trans women to be considered women, her fear of assault, her fear of legal and political confusion. She argues backward from the idea that a person cannot change sex and therefore any recognition of transition as granting membership in a particular category (e.g., transition placing a person in the category of "woman") is a "legal fiction."

But this is just as determinative as the evangelicals before her who say that there is a history and motivation between a person being made into a woman or a man, and therefore, crossing those boundaries is a profound sin. The sin, in Stock's mind, is the evocation of fear in cis women, the upsetting of the supposed binary balance, and the perceived compromise of special legal protected status afforded to women.

American Protestant thought works backward from the idea that we are souls in a body, separate and distinct and at odds with the flesh. Stock works forward from the history of our bodies as determinative for who we must always be, evoking a fear of what could come should we allow our bodies to change in significant ways. For the evangelical, our time with these bodies *must* be spent turning them toward holiness, going against any and all lived experience they may teach us—any fear or anxiety that may arise from within—to bend to the will of God. For the secularist anti-trans feminist, our bodies are shaped by the fear involved in being a woman and the fear of flouting that social role. What they have in common at the end of the day is that phobia, that fear. Stock simply differs in saying that gay people are okay—that is an okay use of the body. Stock herself identifies as a lesbian, and so has simply moved homosexuality out of the realm of "wrong uses for the body" for herself and others like her. But even such work is self-interested and built upon thin ice—when Italy removed non-birthing lesbians from birth certificates in 2023, Stock argued that the "biological reality" of the body does not matter so much in this instance, rather the role that a stable parent plays. Trans men and women, apparently, cannot correctly be fathers and mothers, respectively, but lesbians who played no biological role in their child's creation are mothers. Stock finds herself trapped between a rock and a hard place while she attempts to thread the line between "trans people are not okay" and "lesbians are both mothers." Even in her piece defending her status as a mother, she has to concede to biological narratives about the necessity of a male presence for children in a lesbian household, implying that her own parental role is insufficient (and therefore wrong) for the raising of children, a denial of the proper form of the body.[5] It is impossible to separate the transphobia of the radical feminist from the homophobia of the larger culture.

* * *

In 1998, John Lawrence and Tyron Garner were having sex. This was a normal everyday occurrence for millions of people, and something that typically would go completely unremarked. But on that particular day, a jealous ex-boyfriend of Garner's had called in a report of a man with a weapon antagonizing people in that particular apartment. When police burst in, they found no weapons, but they did find Lawrence, an older white man, in a delicate situation with Garner, a younger black man. Both men were cited under the state's anti-sodomy laws and ordered to pay a fine because what they were doing was illegal under Texas law.

For decades, states had passed laws determining what kinds of sexual acts were allowable within their borders, and they were often applied in uneven ways, punishing gay cisgender men who engaged in the ways gay cis men tend to have sex. Lawrence and Garner appealed the citations they had received, eventually going all the way to the Supreme Court of the United States, which declared sodomy laws as unconstitutional. But such a ruling is in delicate balance—just a little over fifteen years before the 2003 ruling, the same Supreme Court had ruled in the opposite direction in *Bowers v. Hardwick*, in a very similar situation. A police officer decided to serve a warrant that had been invalidated by Hardwick paying a fine weeks earlier, broke into Hardwick's home, and found him having sex with another man. In that case, which landed before the Supreme Court in the year I was born, a 5–4 decision determined that there is no "fundamental right to homosexual sodomy," and therefore, the citation stood, despite being the result of an officer with a homophobic grudge serving an illegal and invalid warrant.

Marginalized and queer bodies have long been subject to extra scrutiny at the hands of the State because of how our bodies differ from the norm. For decades, it was illegal for queer people to have sex under the law. These "sodomy" laws covered everything from anal sex to oral sex without distinguishing the gender of the people performing them (meaning straight people could be punished but never were). Indeed, built into the name of the laws is a peculiarly evangelical interpretation of sexual values from the Bible, named as they are after the sins of Sodom and Gomorrah. The fact that our very laws are named for a particular Christian interpretation of a story from biblical tradition demonstrates just how much influence this fear of the body has had over our culture and our law.

In Genesis 18 and 19, we are told the story of Sodom and Gomorrah, two cities so besieged by wickedness that God promised to destroy them wholly and fully. God tells Abraham of his plans and Abraham asks God to spare the cities if he can find ten righteous within their walls. God sends two angels to destroy Sodom, and they are welcomed into their home by a man named Lot and his family. Men from the city surround the home and demand that the angels be sent out into the city so that the men may "know" them. This is traditionally interpreted by many Protestants and Catholics as an invitation to engage in homosexual acts or some kind of obscene sexual act that would be scandalizing. So strong is this interpretation that Sodom has become shorthand for queer sexuality in general, and sodomy the word for anal sexual activity. Through an evangelical lens, then, the primary sins of Sodom are sexual in nature—men in particular given over to sinful proclivities and horrors. Such a narrow interpretation has become a large part of the basis for the rejection and persecution of the queer community—the Apostle Paul interprets this story as God having given them over to "dishonorable passions" and an abandonment of "natural relations."[6]

Jewish scholars have offered a different interpretation of Sodom, however. There's a midrash—or Jewish commentary—that is told about what the real sin of Sodom is, as summed up by Rabbi Jane Rachel Pitman, the first openly queer woman to be admitted to a rabbinical seminary. She writes:

> According to Jewish tradition, the people of Sodom had a community guesthouse with a single bed. If a guest to the city was too short for the bed, the citizens of Sodom put the person to the rack. If the person too tall, they cut off the guest's feet and legs to fit. . . . The transgression of Sodom wasn't homosexuality but literally and brutally forcing human beings to fit an already existing rigid structure.[7]

Perhaps instead of the sin of Sodom being an extremely specific sexual act, it is the formation of a society that forces people to conform their bodies to a specific way of being, a society that will break you if you do not match their expectations. Perhaps the sin of Sodom is the fear of the body that is embedded in American culture.

Homosexuality is a denial of what our bodies were made to do and evidence of unnatural passions that must be controlled as the sins they are. If your body does not react in the way it is *designed* to do, you must be afraid of it as a specific vector for sin. And if you are reacting outside of the norms of what God has set—outside of heterosexual marriage, outside of a monogamous relationship—then you, too, must be afraid, even if that passion is so-called "natural."

This is the story I was consistently told growing up—our bodies are designed for each other, no matter what other lived experiences or feelings I might have. As such, I lived a great portion of my teenage years thinking that everyone else experienced attraction to women, had to avert their eyes from cleavage, and thought about their same gender in romantic and sexual ways. I genuinely thought that controlling one's flesh and desires meant that everyone else was having to suppress this attraction they felt for all others, including those who shared my then understood identity of woman. Forcing myself to fit into the roles of both woman and heterosexual was, I thought, my burden to bear. And my anxiety kept getting worse and worse. I could not bring my body in line with what was demanded of me—if my body would just comply, everything could be easier.

In the tradition in which I was raised, the body *only* matters when it deviates from a white, cisgender, heterosexual norm. If a person's individuality because of their body sets them apart from the cisgender, heterosexual pathway, that is deemed sin. Central to the belief in the resurrection of the body, of the way the body functions, is the idea that a body's natural, uncorrupted state is white, able-bodied, cisgender, and heterosexual. All else is sin. And this has been the driving force behind most of our cultural homophobia for the last century at least—a fear of that difference in bodies and how we use them. Even without evangelicalism as a broad influence, it is still embedded in the way we talk about bodies and their differences from the norm.

Dr. Omri Elisha, an anthropologist who teaches at the City University of New York, has written about this peculiar evangelical belief where the body is determinist and central but also a thing to be conquered, as mentioned in chapter 1. Elisha has spent much of his career examining the lives of evangelicals and how they interact with the world around them. Because the body is a locus of sin that prevents true connection for evangelicals, Elisha argues, the conversion experience of the average Christian is one of giving up the body to the indwelling of the spirit, of bending one's bodily experience to the life of God's knowledge and Truth, regardless of what we as individuals may bring to the table through our lived experience. This theology, Elisha writes, positions evangelicalism as anti-intellectual in its very nature, summed up by what one of his compatriots at the Bible study he attended said: "God tells us only what we need to know. He doesn't have to provide all the story details in order for the Gospel to make sense. God wants us to move toward him by faith. The only people who are really concerned with the complicated factual stuff are atheists, and there's nothing you can say to convince them anyway."[8]

God's will and agency are centralized in the evangelical sphere; therefore, it would make sense that a body that does not comply—a body that responds to attraction differently, or a body that produces dysphoric pain—must be molded into compliance. Gay people who embrace the fact that they are gay are merely being ruled by their bodies. Trans people, likewise, are delusional in the idea that changing their bodies could possibly solve any problems. Because any internal lived experience is deemed secondary to the emptying out of one's self for Christ, to be subsumed by the divine will, any view that prioritizes embodiment, that listens to the body is sinful.

All of this coming to a head in the twenty-first century now can be attributed to the strong influence of white Protestantism on American culture since its founding. Though there are pockets here and there of differing beliefs, particularly propounded by people who are existing in the margins—Black people, queer people, disabled people—the dominant cultural attitude is one of a body that is merely a flesh suit for the true person, for the soul inhabiting it. It is a house—a temple—and seeking to radically alter it except for cases of disease or damage evokes intense fear. Culture has developed a normative ideal that proclaims the self as separate from the body, even if it does not take a particular evangelical bent of divine influence. Even in the language of discussing bodies, we separate our self from them—"my body is doing this" or "my body won't let me do that." The body and the "I" inhabiting it are two separate entities, and we must control our bodies lest they lead us down the wrong path.

For queer and trans people, this fear plays a role in our own bodies. The person whose body fits into the normative structures of society—the expected heterosexual and cisgender—naturally follows a developmental path that we all know: childhood to adolescence to adulthood. This path is common and culturally understood throughout American culture—teenagehood is when you find your first love, you experiment some in college, and then you settle down by thirty. Part of the ways in which we classify bodies and understand cultural moments is built upon this idea that even if people are different individually, we all follow this same basic path.

For LGBT people, that path often gets interrupted. We often realize our difference early on but because of cultural pressures and both external and internal fear about what being different *means*, our first time through teenager-dom as an actual teenager can be a false or stunted growth period as we work to either conform to the heterosexual, cisgender culture we are told we should be or spend time coming to terms with our own identities. For many, the onset of puberty produces immense fear, as our own body betrays us in ways we did not expect or were not emotionally prepared for. Numerous trans people have written about how they were surprised by their own puberty because internally, they thought, "well, I'm X so obviously my body is going to develop in these ways" and then reacted with fear and surprise when it didn't. This isn't to say these trans people were somehow naive about their own development but rather that they lacked access to adequate information and health care to understand why their body was misbehaving.

As a result, many, many LGBT people go through what is called a second adolescence. In our twenties or even thirties, when we become adults and are able to be independent of the familial world in which we grew up, we finally find community that can know us for who we really are for the first time. And then we go through a lot of "firsts" that should've happened in adolescence but now happen in adulthood—first kisses, first relationships, first sexual experiences, first break-ups, first time feeling confident and beautiful in the mirror, first time exploring what one's own body can do. Fear holds us back as teenagers, and it is only after we have learned that our bodies are not things to fear but rather to be embraced that we can grow into our very selves.

As a queer, trans person, my process of coming into my own was deeply delayed by my own fear and disconnect from my bodily self. I was born in the 1980s and became an adult in the 2000s. The first presidential election that I could vote in was 2004—an election where the question of marriage equality for LGBT individuals was a primary issue in the campaign. By that time, I was aware that I was different, but I was so terrified of what that meant that I suppressed any and all thoughts or ideas of my sexuality or gender. I veiled myself in ignorance of my own body, of my own flesh, because I was so afraid to come out to myself.

This fear of my own body was all consuming for years. I thought I needed to set aside my desire to be in a relationship, my desire to be held and loved by a person who saw me for who I was, my desire to be seen as a human capable of loving. I tried, metaphorically, to "die to self"—to kill my sense of selfhood so that God could increase, so that God could take over instead. Omri Elisha describes this very phenomenon in the megachurches he studied:

> Evangelicals measure themselves by the standards of a kind of inner-worldly asceticism that prioritizes personal revelation while at the same time disciplines the self to increase its reliance on the

agency of God, as well as on the moral guidance and fellowship of like-minded Christians.[9]

This pressure (both internal and external) that happens in evangelical spaces is multiplied for those of us in the LGBT community, because the *expectation* is of straight cisgender ideals and those who do not match up will deny the self to be straight and cis for Christ. In 2017, this conception was reaffirmed when the Council for Biblical Manhood and Womanhood issued the Nashville Statement, which was then signed by several important evangelical voices of the day, including Karen Swallow-Prior, William Lane Craig, Albert Mohler and Russell Moore from the SBC, and R. C. Sproul. The statement declared that it is impossible for a faithful Christian to be homosexual or transgender:

> WE AFFIRM that self-conception as male or female should be defined by God's holy purposes in creation and redemption as revealed in Scripture. WE DENY that adopting a homosexual or transgender self-conception is consistent with God's holy purposes in creation and redemption.[10]

To be a faithful Christian, then, is to deny all parts of oneself that might indicate a non-straight, non-cisgender identity. The body matters only insofar as it indicates who God created you to be, but you better discipline and control it to match that role—otherwise you're an unrepentant sinner.

This is the center of the phobia of the body, the fear that bodies might not precisely reflect the hierarchical structures man believes they do. And it's the heart of the homophobia, queerphobia, and transphobia that has resulted in State-mandated restrictions on human bodies. People who do not conform readily must be *made* to conform, through State-sanctioned violence if need be. But what is that fear of, precisely? What sits at the root of that fear?

Feminist scholar Catherine MacKinnon, who has been vocal within the feminist movement as a lawyer and activist for decades, spoke to this in relationship to transgender people at a conference at the University of Oxford in November 2022, followed up with an article in the journal *Signs*. She writes that the problem is not and never was the body itself but a fearful social hierarchy that is laid over top of that biology. Speaking in relationship to women's bodies, she writes:

> Women are not, in fact, subordinated or oppressed by our bodies. We do not need to be liberated from our chromosomes or our ovaries. It is core male-dominant ideology that attributes the source of women's inequality to our nature, our biological sex, which for male dominance makes it inevitable, immutable, unchangeable, on us. As if our bodies, rather than male dominant social systems, do it to us. It is as if Black people's melanin content is the cause of police violence against them, rather than the meaning police attribute to their appearance (racial markers in this instance) and the law and culture of impunity for their actions. If women's oppression is defined by what defines women, and that is our sexed biology as this group defines it, the very most we can change is the excesses of male power. Never male power itself.[11]

Returning to the body, determining the body as a primary voice in determining one's role in life, plays into the work of misogyny. It is not our bodies that exempt or oppress us—it is the social meaning of those bodies, the hierarchy imposed upon us from the outside, that fears complexity and free will in determining what one's body is, does, and means.

Baptized in this fear is a desire to rid oneself of uncertainty, to have answers to what it *means* to be human. Transgender identity, in particular, offends the sensibility that what you are born as is the thing in which you must stay. When I speak to people who "disagree" with transgender identity, I often find that they are expressing a deep-seated fear of the idea that our biology does not have to remain our destiny. Many women, for instance, have found deep comfort in the narrative that God has designed them for a life of staying at home, mothering children, and making dinner for a husband who is working to support the family. Many secular anti-trans women find great comfort in the idea that they are merely trapped in their role in society by accident of birth, and that the lines around what it means to be a woman must be held in our bodies and, nihilistically, we can't change that circumstance of birth. It's very comforting, set, and secure. Your path is laid out for you, and it becomes easy to be who you are supposed to be. Your body is an accident of birth, and that is the only thing that matters.

The trans and queer body being allowed to exist, being accepted, demonstrates the lie of safe and secure and set for what it is; if it is possible that God created me to be non-binary and queer and I can co-create myself, then the rules we all have been following, the things we believe to be capital-T Truth, might not actually be true. It would mean that our bodies are not destiny. To both the conservative Christian and the anti-trans feminist, the body is a *rule*, instructions to be followed throughout one's life. Regardless of who you grow to be, your body is a set of instructions that are built into who you are—and changing your body is out of the question, ever.

In all cases, the trans and queer body is set as an object to fear— that our body could at once be the seat of our selfhood *and* a site to change and challenge the normative is profoundly scary to a white culture that wants people in neat little categorical boxes. But the fun part of those boxes is that they're human inventions, and as such can be changed. The fear evoked by the self-determination of an LGBT body should instead be redirected into an understanding of bodies as wildly elastic, malleable. They are our homes, sure, but we are free to decorate them as we wish.

7 | THE ECONOMIC BODY

In the mid-twentieth century, the electronics company General Electric got a new CEO. Jack Welch was concerned about nothing more than money and status. When he first joined the company, he was so disappointed to learn that all of his coworkers had received the same raise that he did that he badgered his boss into giving him a larger raise, because Jack felt he deserved it. In his first managerial role, in the Research and Development department at GE, he pushed his researchers so hard that they ended up causing an explosion at the factory trying to develop a new plastic. But, as is the story with many a white man, Jack continued to fail upward until he was handpicked to be the next CEO of what was then one of the biggest companies in the United States.

Even that didn't satisfy him. He insisted that he could be better than other CEOs, could bring in more profits. And he did so, by bringing in layoffs to temporarily boost stock share prices by making the company look like it was making more money on paper. Eventually, GE started shuttering research divisions, no longer the innovator of goods and products that people would use in their homes. Instead they began working in financial services, turning GE into something of a bank. By the time Jack left as CEO, around 40% of GE's output was in financial services and the company had laid off hundreds of thousands of employees.

In 1995, at 60 years old and five years from retirement, Jack suffered his first heart attack. He underwent a quintuple bypass. During the time between the heart attack and surgery, Jack reached out to people he knew who had undergone similar surgery—Henry Kissinger and then Disney CEO, Michael Eisner. According to Eisner, he expressed immense fear at the prospect of dying.

But a few years later, when Stuart Varney of PBS asked him about his brush with death: "Was that a real change in life for you? A change in perhaps your spiritual approach?" Jack simply responded, "No." Not even a chance at death would shake his iron fist. When pressed on his answer, he eventually responded that he regretted not spending more. Not buying that $100 bottle of wine and instead settling for cheaper. If there was one thing he would do, it would be to *spend spend spend*.[1]

But those who knew him knew the narrative he had built for himself was different from who he was in those vulnerable moments when death was a very real possibility. According to witnesses, he was begging for the doctors to save him, to do everything in their power to keep him from the grave.

Jack Welch eventually made it to eighty-four years old, finally passing just weeks before the COVID-19 pandemic shut down the entire country. It's unclear if he ever learned anything more than "I regret not spending enough money." General Electric, the company he helmed for a couple decades, has become a shell of its former self. It went from being one of the top-rated places to work to having a company culture rated as "not successful" by most employees in surveys from Indeed.

What happened to change the culture during Welch's tenure as CEO was a relatively simple but very important transformation. When Welch became CEO, he wanted to make GE more profitable than ever before, and he prioritized short-term gains. That meant that boosting stock for shareholders was a primary motivation, and the way to do that was making GE look like it was making money *on paper*. The easiest way to show a profit on paper? Cut labor. Welch instituted massive layoffs across the company to boost profit revenue—by cutting out labor costs. Prior to Welch instituting layoffs as a profit-making strategy, they were commonly only used when a company was struggling or if costs demanded it. Welch shifted the criteria to "anything that makes the profit look better and bigger."

This meant families that had depended on GE's job security, benefits, and pension were suddenly cut loose, often at ages where finding a new job with equal or better benefits was nigh on impossible. In several areas across the United States, Welch's layoff moves killed entire towns, forcing people to move locations in order to find new work. But Welch never felt the sting—his CEO compensation got bigger and his benefits more lavish while families across the United States had to change their entire life plan because of these layoffs.

For Jack, these families were just numbers on a spreadsheet. It didn't matter that stomachs would literally go hungry, that entire lives were uprooted.

This is the economic body.

For better or worse, we live under a capitalist system—one that is currently wildly unequal in its distribution of wealth: people whose wealth is nearing a quarter of a trillion have immense power, while nurses who pull double shifts on their feet all day have to argue with their employers in order to get fair pay. The ways our bodies are applied to this thing called "work" are wildly unequal, and there was no better example of that division than during the COVID-19 pandemic.

One of the last things I did before the pandemic actually began shutting things down worldwide was to go for birthday drinks with my friends. A bar that was something of a speakeasy behind a popular restaurant here in Minneapolis was hosting an entirely new menu of mocktails using non-alcoholic spirits. I haven't had alcohol in about a decade because I'm on meds that make it fairly unwise to combine with depressants, so I was excited to have actual multiple options for drinks that were creative and fun without alcohol. My friends and I crammed eight of us into a six-person booth and shared drinks and snacks throughout the night. Everyone was close, huddled together, occasionally handing a neighbor our drink with "here, try this! It's so good!" I took photos of the menu so I could try to recreate some of them at home. It was my first time getting to taste anything with a gin-esque flavor, and I was falling in love. Maybe I could be a fake gin and tonic person? I decided I needed to come back once I got the new job I was interviewing for.

Two weeks later, the country mostly shut down. It's inappropriate to call it a lockdown, because we could still leave the house, stores were open, and we could go places. But it was *different*. Many of my friends who had office jobs had to learn to balance remote working and remote schooling, as their children were home all day alongside them. My teacher friends had to change everything almost overnight to start teaching remotely. Restaurants closed while they tried to figure out how to shift to delivery and take-out-only businesses.

But service workers never had any of that luxury. Some places offered hazard pay initially, but as it became clear it would be at least a year before vaccines would be available, that hazard pay slowly dried up. And service or manufacturing industry workers by and large couldn't work from home—it's a little hard to do the work of making a person their morning coffee if you're not physically present at the espresso machine.

The first community spread I knew of in Minneapolis could be traced back to a worker at a local co-op grocery store. In those early days, we spoke of it with fear, tracking where cases were spreading and where it was going—and by and large, it was either the wealthy, who had been traveling and brought it back with them, or those people whose bodies were in contact with the public every single day for hours a day.

In my hometown, the first major outbreak was at a meat-processing plant where the employees are mostly black and brown immigrants. The plant has been a staple of the economy in Sioux Falls my entire life. The plant, originally owned by the Morrell & Co meat-processing company, was bought out by Smithfield foods in 1995, though it took a long time for the town to switch from calling it Morrell's to Smithfield's. "Meat processing" is a banal euphemism for what happens there. Pigs from the across the nation are shipped in, where they are killed and then workers butcher them into smaller cuts of meat and ground product for packaging and selling in grocery stores. The smell from the literally thousands of animals that go through that plant makes it very pungent—with the right wind, you could smell it across the entire city.

Older factories like the Smithfield one in Sioux Falls are at particular risk for COVID outbreaks spreading rapidly through the plant. The design of the factory itself puts the workers literally shoulder to shoulder as they work. Because they had not shut down with the initial news of the pandemic (South Dakota's state government steadfastly refused to take any COVID mitigation measures), the plant became the site of one of the first major outbreaks in the United States. Within a month of the start of the public health emergency, nearly a thousand infections and two deaths were linked to the plant.[2] At that point, it was the largest outbreak tied to a single location in the entire country.

The first death was a man named Augustín Rodriguez, who was one year away from retirement. He was sixty-four and had worked at the plant since moving to the United States from El Salvador with his wife, Angelita, about twenty years prior. He was a quiet, churchgoing man who loved to surprise his wife with her favorite flowers—gardenias—or finding just the perfect piece of fruit. He caught

COVID during the initial outbreak, which Smithfield had responded to without any staffing changes but instead with an offer of a $500 bonus if an employee didn't miss a shift in April. This perverse incentive resulted in COVID rates skyrocketing throughout the plant.

In November 2021, Smithfield was ordered to pay just $13,394 in fines for their failure to respond adequately to the COVID outbreak and protecting their employees. And that $13,394 is little comfort for Angelita Rodriguez, who lost her husband that April. In the local newspaper article about the death, Angelita said plainly that her husband had been worked to death:

> "I lost him because of that horrible place," said Angelita, 73, through a translator. "Those horrible people and their supervisors, they're sitting in their homes, and they're happy with their families."[3]

Her husband became a sacrifice to the never-ending demand of work. His body was subject to the whims of capitalism, who encouraged workers to come in sick during a pandemic so that production would not be slowed. While the executives and managers worked from their home office, the factory workers stood shoulder to shoulder, unable to avoid spreading a deadly contagion, day in and day out, their bodies becoming grist for the capitalist mill.

But even before the pandemic, workers often suffered for their jobs. There's a saying that every safety regulation is written in blood. Before the advent of regulating bodies like OSHA, it was extremely common for workers in factories to lose limbs or suffer permanent disability or even death from workplaces not having safety regulations. Lock out tag out procedures for heavy machinery, for example, happened because without them, workers risked machines being turned on while they were inside them, with disastrous results. Even basic things like fire safety and safe exits from a building had to be fought for, often after blood had already been spilled.

On a Saturday in March 1911, just as the workday in the Triangle Shirtwaist Factory was coming to a close, a fire sparked up in a bin holding hundreds of scraps of fabric. It was likely from a cigarette or an improperly extinguished match. In an environment covered in fabric and wood, the fire spread quickly. With no warning systems, people on the floor above learned of the fire only when it reached their floor. The workers desperately tried to escape, but the stairwell doors were locked—a measure taken to prevent workers from taking unauthorized breaks, which likely is what led to people smoking on the floor in the first place. The foreman with the key to the stairwell fled the fire, leaving over a hundred workers trapped. As workers piled onto a rickety fire escape stairway attached to the outside of the building, it warped from the weight and the heat of the fire, spilling more than a dozen bodies on the sidewalk a hundred feet below. Sixty-two more, desperate to escape a fiery death, jumped from the eighth- and ninth-floor windows. All told, 146 people—123 of them women and children—perished in the fire.

Rose Schneiderman, a Polish immigrant and union activist, spoke at the memorial for the victims of the fire, lamenting the fact that the public ignored the plight of workers and disapproved of union movements:

> I would be a traitor to these poor burned bodies if I came here to talk good fellowship. We have tried you good people of the public and we have found you wanting. . . . I can't talk fellowship to you who are gathered here. Too much blood has been spilled. I know from my experience it is up to the working people to save themselves. The only way they can save themselves is by a strong working-class movement.[4]

While the pandemic was perhaps not as visceral as a fire engulfing two floors of a high-rise in the middle of the day, it was just as horrifying for workers. Over a million people in the United States died, as workers begged for hazard pay, mandated masking, and sick leave to avoid spreading a deadly virus. At one point, the job with the highest death rate was that of line cooks—an average worker in your average restaurant, decimated by a deadly virus. And companies often did nothing more than installing plastic windows that did nothing to keep germs out and refusing to give employees any authority to enforce mask policies, if they even existed.

In American culture, we're very resistant to seeing labor as selling one's body. In fact, a strong capitalist, Protestant work ethic streak has prevented many of us from seeing the work we do for money as involving our bodies at all, especially for "white collar" office workers. We also tend to reject the idea that our bodies matter at all for the work we produce, even though bias studies have repeatedly shown that the same material coming from, say, a Black woman, is received with more critique than when it comes from a white man. Work culture—especially upper middle class working culture—likes to pretend bodies do not have any impact on the work that is mostly the product of the mind. This is the basis of the American meritocracy—that your hard work and smarts are what will win the day, not who you happen to be in your body. It's colorblind, judging you solely on your merit, not the body you possess—a prime incarnation of this white Anglo-Saxon dualism that pretends bodies don't matter at all.

But meritocracy has never actually been true—it's simply another way in which dualism has pretended that bodies don't matter. Historically, women—no matter what brain power they possessed—were kept from the workforce and from education by structural barriers that prevented them from receiving education equal to that of cisgender men, and then their lack of knowledge about specific topics is cited as evidence of their natural inferiority. The same thing happened with BIPOC throughout our nation's history, where Black people in particular were structurally prevented from being literate, and therefore, since they could not prove their mind's capabilities on a playing field that was deeply favorable to educated white men, such things were held to be part of their natural inferiority. Entire branches of science, such as phrenology, arose to explain away these racial differences that actually came from structural, systemic prejudice.

One primary example that is still a problem today is school funding. For that, we have to go back to the 1940s and the GI Bill. Following the war effort in World War II, white soldiers who had fought overseas returned home and were able to purchase homes thanks to subsidies from the federal government. Homeownership is one of the primary mechanisms for building wealth across generations, because houses and land tend to appreciate and grow in value, allowing a person who bought a cheap home in 1950 to sell it twenty years later for a much higher profit. But the benefits of these bills were only available to white families—Black soldiers who had served were denied such benefits. Cheap homes for white people also came alongside a discriminatory practice called "redlining," where Black people who could afford homes were restricted to certain neighborhoods in cities, ghettoized into areas deemed "less desirable" and concentrating poverty in specific over-policed areas.

The Civil Rights Movement of the 1950s and 1960s pushed back against this as discriminatory practice, fighting first for school integration so that white and Black kids were attending the same schools, and then fighting for other advances like the Voting Rights Act, which guaranteed the right to vote, and the Civil Rights Act, which guaranteed protection against discrimination based on race or sex. This was followed up by the Fair Housing Act, which outlawed redlining and block busting—a practice where a realtor will go around to a white neighborhood and talk about how the neighborhood's going downhill since all those Black people moved in and surely you'd like a nicer home out in the whiter suburbs?

But even with the Fair Housing Act and numerous discriminatory practices outlawed, the presence of Black people in a neighborhood still resulted in property valuations that are lower than in all-white neighborhoods, despite all other factors being basically the same. This can artificially suppress the property taxes paid by a neighborhood—which fund schools. So majority-Black neighborhoods, regardless of the incomes and the actual composition of the people who live there, are more likely to have poorer schools that lack funds simply because of artifacts of racism in property valuation. And poorly funded schools lead to fewer opportunities for education and advancement.

A person born into those circumstances will have a hard time overcoming it without a lot of luck. But the American belief in meritocracy, which prioritizes the amorphous disembodied mind over that of the physical body, says that hard work and dedication should be enough to overcome the disadvantages of poor schooling and depressed economies. It's the story I told myself for ages—I am successful because I am smart and I know I am smart because I did well at school. But the reality is, I was the white child of two teachers who lived in a fairly well-to-do area, went to a well-funded school, and thrived in a school environment where the goal was to regurgitate information in specific ways. When I left that structure for the white collar working world, I struggled immensely. Turns out, when you're neurodivergent, the continually changing grind of school that has a defined endpoint can artificially inflate your own opinion of how you handle work!

It took me a bit to realize that I can't skate by on being smart, because my intelligence is only possible because of who I happened to be born to and where I grew up. I have a college degree and two master's degrees, both of which are from well-respected universities (one of which is repeatedly named a top university in the world). And that access was possible because I grew up with two white parents who grew up in a system that rewarded people not for being hard workers or being good at their jobs, but rather, for simply being white. My father's economic life story—the first of seven born to a hair dresser and a mechanic in the 1950s—was made possible because of their bodies existing in this category we call white. It is inescapable.

The cultural dualism, which creates a meritocracy that ignores bodies in reality, also has created a middle class where bodies are not counted in labor, though a nonworking, disabled body is easily dismissed as having no value to a capitalist society. But as Studs Terkel cataloged so brilliantly in his oral history, *Working*, bodies are integral to work. Terkel was a Jewish writer who was born in New York and grew up in Chicago. He hosted a radio show in the Chicago area for many decades and wrote numerous books that were essentially transcribed interviews with people from all walks of life. In *Working*, he talked to people about their jobs, and in one memorable exchange—revealed to the world in its original form through audio recordings of the interview—a factory worker talks about automation machines that were brought into the plant:

> Well, it looks like a robot, you know? And it reminds me of a praying mantis. When they took the Unimates on, we were building 60 an hour prior to the Unimates. And when we came back to work with the Unimates, we were building 101 cars per hour. See, they never tire. They never sweat. They never complain. They never miss work. They're always there.[5]

Gary Bryner and Terkel talk about the "assembly line" approach being "dependent upon the fact each guy's exactly like the other guy." All bodies are treated as interchangeable cogs in a machine. But Bryner, the factory worker he's speaking with, says that clearly that's not true:

> You know, they use the stopwatches. And they say, look; we know from experience that it takes so many seconds to walk from here to there. We know that it takes so many seconds to shoot that screw. We know the gun turns so fast and the screw's so long and the hole's so deep. We know how long it takes. And that's what that guy's going to do. And our argument has always been, you know, that's mechanical. That's not human. Look; we tire. We sweat.

117

We have hangovers. We have upset stomachs. We have feelings, emotions. And we're not about to be placed in a category of a machine.[6]

Bryner didn't intend to be a union man, but it turned out to be the best way he knew to articulate a fundamental fact obvious to him back in the 1960s: men aren't machines and cannot be made to act as them. Our bodies *matter* for the very fact that we have needs and wants and humanity. And that means not every process can be optimized and not everything can be shaved down to the precise second. No matter what work we are doing, we exist in bodies that will make us stop when stopping is called for, regardless of the situation.

I've had a number of job interviews in my life and rarely turned down opportunities that came up. But one time, I ended an interview early when a company explained how scheduling and shifts worked in their organization. It was a glorified call center position, doing customer service work for a business security company (I was desperate to find something for a job). And the Human Resources person doing the phone screen explained that every day would be scheduled down to the minute, including bathroom breaks and lunch. I went silent for what must've been only about five or seven seconds but felt like an eternity in the moment. Finally I struggled to say, "That . . . that does not sound like the environment for me." And I ended the interview. I wasn't *that* desperate.

That job wanted to control my body, to the point where I had no say over basic bodily functions. And while that environment is perhaps an extreme example, it illustrates the fact that even labor that is primarily office work does, in fact, involve one's body. No matter what you do for a paycheck, you are selling your body for it, and even if your primary output is writing, or intellectual exercise, or thought, it is still constrained by and affected by your body, because you are a bodymind, not some amorphous soul.

I started a new job in 2023. It's a day job working for a non-profit doing grant work. It's almost entirely work from home—I'm in the office once every couple of weeks and attend events on weekends as needed to support the development team. Working from home has made me more, not less, aware of my body and its needs. I take fewer sick days now because symptoms that would ordinarily make it impossible to commute to an office are fine when all I'm doing at home is sitting on the computer in my pajamas. Being able to control the temperature of my environment, when I use the bathroom, and when and what I eat is part and parcel of the caretaking of my body necessary to make my work possible. I have access to all the meds I need if my allergies get bad mid-day. I can take Tums if breakfast gives me heartburn. I can change up my meals if I need to. And I can do basic chores like laundry and cleaning in between meetings, which means I'm not trying to cram those chores into the evening or weekend.

Even with the best of circumstances, though, I am still selling my body for the work of others. All of us are. Our bodies, inseparable from our minds and thus our work, are vital to the project of capitalism. And that in itself is not necessarily bad, but it becomes so when the exchange of the labor for money becomes deeply unequal. CEOs do not perform four hundred times more labor than the lowest paid person in their company, and yet their position is rewarded as though they do. And companies have repeatedly reduced their employees to numbers on a spreadsheet, depersonalizing and dehumanizing the very real human bodies that drive productivity. But it is the bodies of those who labor that have the most power.

This kind of treatment is why we are currently living in a resurgence of a workers' movement. Growing up conservative in South Dakota, unions were something I was told about in negative terms, with my parents refusing to join the teachers union, and other teachers feeling free to air their opinions about the union (always negative) in class. I heard a lot of times that union meant that bad teachers couldn't be fired, that workers who didn't deserve it would get the same pay as everyone else, and that unions made it impossible to operate business in the free market.

But in reality, unions have long kept workers' rights from being trampled, ensuring dignity and autonomy within the workspace because of the backing of unions. In light of the Smithfield company's poor practices during the COVID-19 pandemic, the union for the meatpackers renegotiated their contract, instituting higher pay and the right to have a leave of absence of up to three weeks without the threat of losing your job or pay for that time period. The union specifically cited both that the majority of workers are immigrants who occasionally need time to return to their home countries for visits and the results of the COVID-19 outbreaks as reasons for asking for those specific measures.

Unions give the workers power in an inherently unbalanced system. A friend of mine who works at a local Starbucks that voted to unionize in 2022 told me that a big reason they did so was to regain some negotiating power in that relationship. For my friend, the union isn't—as the company would have you believe—an antagonistic group but rather a demonstration of commitment to the work and of investment in the career. In a lot of service industries, because the *job* treats the workers as disposable, the workers begin to see themselves as disposable. And unionizing is the opportunity to ask for a better environment that doesn't treat workers as disposable cogs. It comes from the management on equal footing and from a strong negotiation position that puts the reality of the workers' bodies back into the equation.

For the Starbucks union, Starbucks Workers United, for example, union workers have demands beyond basic economic conditions like pay and more sick leave. It also asks for basic non-discrimination protections not only from fellow employees, but the right to respect from customers of the store. So often, food service workers have to put up with being treated like they aren't people, and one change the Starbucks union seeks is to allow workers to refuse service, to defend themselves without retaliation from management. Simple safety measures that workers have been denied because their bodies are seen as interchangeable and disposable are being won back because workers unionized and demanded to be treated as people.

During the writing of this manuscript, the Writers Guild of America (WGA) went on strike to push for better streaming residuals and protections against the replacement of their jobs with terrible artificial intelligence robots. The studios refused to negotiate on many vital aspects, so a strike was approved by the union almost universally. What has been notable about this strike was just how physical it is: people were out on the line, marching in front of studio offices and studio lots, day in and day out. It was not a matter of simply refusing to work, but actively, physically, involving yourself in stopping the work of others. One early strategy was engaging other unions who were not technically on strike but had rules saying they cannot cross a picket line. So early in the mornings, WGA members—even just one or two—would show up at the studio lot doors and create a picket line, which the other union workers could not and would not cross. No physical bodies on the line: no strike. Even though writing is largely intellectual work, fighting for fair pay and equal rights in a capitalist system is deeply, deeply physical. And the CEOs and bosses and studio heads fear that physicality, fear the power of just one or two people with a sign standing outside the studio lot before the 7 a.m. call time.

Because we are selling our bodies for labor, those bodies have a lot of power. And management is afraid of that—management is afraid we will take our bodies seriously enough, care for them enough, to desire protections for ourselves. Recognizing that our bodies *matter* terrifies management because it means those bodies can walk out and won't behave like machines. The inequality depends on those at the bottom continuing to cooperate with the dehumanization of their very selves—and refusing to do so is the best way to make change.

8 | THE DYING BODY

One of the best gifts my mother ever gave our family was her death. I know that sounds morbid, but inasmuch as a person can have a good death, my mother did. She fell ill in November 2013, rushed to the hospital from urgent care after she went in with symptoms of a heart attack. The doctors put stents in, and we expected her to get better and recover by Christmas.

She didn't. That early hospital trip was the start of a months-long journey of Mom slowly succumbing to a mysterious illness that took her appetite, her ability to move around, and eventually, her life. It took months to finally get the diagnosis of amyloidosis, which was leading to multiple organ failure. Toward the end of May 2014, the family gathered together and discussed options with Mom's doctors. The treatment would require an extended trip to the Mayo Clinic in Rochester, MN—a four-hour drive from home—and did not have a great chance of success, as the illness had already progressed so far.

Mom looked around the room at all of us and said, "I'm ready to go." Not to Rochester. Not to Mayo Clinic. But instead, to die. The palliative care team came in and talked the family through what the next few weeks would look like as Mom would move to hospice care. She would be at home, with her cat, being cared for by her family as long as we could.

The last week, she was moved into the hospital for a constant morphine drip as the pain was getting to be too much. The last words I heard from her were calling out my dad's name as the nurses moved her to her hospital bed and accidentally jostled her awake. She cried out, "Larry!" in a scared voice and he grabbed her hand and let her know that he was right there. A few days later, she died.

I stopped in at the hospital to be with my dad in the moments before the orderlies took the body away. The mother I'd kissed on the forehead that morning before I left to run errands was lifeless, slack-jawed and unmoving on her hospital bed. No one had yet covered her with a blanket or hid her death mask from the world. I buried my face in my dad's shoulder so I would not have to see.

A week later, I showed up at the funeral home where she had been taken and embalmed. Her lips had been glued together and her eyelids glued shut. Subtle makeup had been put on to hide the pallor of death, and she had been changed from a hospital gown into one of her favorite comfortable shirts and jeans. I was struck by how she simply looked to be asleep—but for the lack of her chest rising up and down to indicate breath, you would be entirely forgiven if you did think she was merely resting. That is, until I walked up to the casket to say goodbye. I reached out and touched her hands, folded one on top of the other above her heart.

And I immediately recoiled, surprised by their chill. I knew intellectually that she was gone but it was not real until that moment of touch where I reached for *her*, for her body, and was not met with the warmth of blood flowing through the veins but instead with a chill carried from a refrigerated storeroom for bodies. It snapped that uncanny valley into focus, and brought to the forefront the very fact that the person I had known as my mom had ceased to be. She was no longer reachable in any manner available to me here.

Death in American culture is strange. We're not good at it. And I think that's by and large because Americans—many culturally Protestant, existing constantly in this morass of heaven/hell dichotomies—are scared at the end of the day about what it means. We're scared about what it means for us, for our loved ones, for the world after we go, because it is the ultimate unknown. Even if we get comfortable with the fact that our bodies change and age, there is still a part of us that is afraid of death. So we have created cultural boundaries around death that distance us from the reality of the dead body.

In 1997, several psychologists compiled a handbook for doctors and others in the medical field to work to understand death and dying as it is approached in non-Western cultures. In an essay, Paul C. Rosenblatt writes: "There are no pan-human categories for understanding death; how people think about death is everywhere culturally embedded."[1] As an example of this, Rosenblatt brings up the Toraja of Sulawesi in Indonesia, an indigenous culture that has a total population of around 1.1 million. In this culture, the death of a loved one is not an immediate act that happens in one moment but an extended period from the point of physical death. The body is kept in the house with the family until the date of the funeral, which may be weeks away. And before the actual funeral date, the deceased is not referred to as such—rather, they are "sleeping."[2] The funeral itself takes place over many days, involving the slow movement of the deceased's body from the house to the gravesite with very specific dress and rituals. The husband will still sleep next to his wife's dead body during this time. The person is not fully dead—not really, not completely—until the grief rituals are complete.

Such rituals are often considered strange by westerners for whom death has meant a body whisked away by professionals, washed and cleaned away from any prying eyes, and preserved. Funerals happen within a week here. But as Rosenblatt points out, "it is easier to believe the proper beliefs, follow the proper rituals and feel the proper feelings when everyone agrees that they are proper."[3] For many in the West, quick disposal of the body is considered proper, while for others a slow transition allowing for grief is more appropriate.

Elisabeth Kubler-Ross, a psychiatrist, summarized death and grieving into five stages of denial, anger, bargaining, depression, and finally, acceptance. Kubler-Ross's ideas have become so universal in English-speaking society that it is generally accepted as a truism regardless of your background. The stages of grief, while not linear, are something we *all* go through.

Except: we don't. Other sociologists and psychiatrists working around the time Kubler-Ross became popular have critiqued her perspective as universalizing a uniquely Western and Protestant society.[4] Philosopher Walter Kaufmann points out that while she places denial as the first stage, she does not delineate between cultural preference or universal truth, as many of the hundreds of interviews she conducted do not actually contain denial or reactions that include such. Sociologist Jane Littlewood takes this idea a little bit further, arguing (with hindsight that Kaufmann did not have access to in 1976) that the universalizing of such stages may, in fact, create a feed-back loop wherein people—medical professionals, in particular—are *expected* to engage in a cultural ritual of denial in order to match the cultural expectations. This results in a deepening of the grief process because people are made to feel like they are grieving "wrong" if their emotional reaction does not match the westernized, cultural version we are all expected to mimic.

It's even harder in a deeply dualistic society, where Protestant conceptions of death make it harder to talk about and mourn because there is a lingering question of what happens to the person after the death and the afterlife. Death is mourned in many families as a neces-sary evil, a result of the fall of Man into sin, and, potentially, a punish-ment for failure to live a good life when on Earth.

My first memorable encounter with death was in high school. In the debate circuit, coaches, students, and people who volunteer as judges at tournaments tend to form a close-knit family—after all, you spend school year after school year seeing these same people at tournaments every weekend from October to March. It's understandable that you'd get to know them. One judge and assistant coach was a student at one of our state colleges in South Dakota. During a college party at which he had been drinking, he stumbled backward down the staircase to the basement of the house and slammed his head into the concrete. He died as a result of his injuries. He was only twenty years old.

At the next debate tournament that was held, there was a moment at the awards ceremony of tribute to the young man. I was a Bible-thumping evangelical at the time and assumed that anyone who did not believe as I did was going to hell. So when the speaker said, "He's looking down on us now," I quietly scoffed. I knew enough to know that judging a person in the time of mourning following their death was a bad idea but lacked the empathy to avoid actually doing it. At that time, I viewed his death as righteous punishment for his behavior while alive—a tragic accident became righteous punishment for not honoring his body and his role in the world. And now he would suffer for eternity.

This was obviously a cruel and unhealthy way to approach death, but it was not out of line for what my culture had taught me at the time. For me, it made sense to imagine that the body that failed to comply with the rigid rules for right living in life would need to be punished in death. But for people mourning, it was important to imagine that his death was not the end of his story. We both saw the afterlife as a path to implement our own ideals—mine out of cruelty and contempt for nonbelievers, and theirs out of grief for the friend they had lost. At the end of the day, both narratives were mechanisms for comforting ourselves in the face of the unknown. Rather than dealing with the finality of that moment, many of us reach for ways to talk around death, to talk about the dead as if they have continued on elsewhere. Funerals are for the living, after all.

In 1955, the sociologist Geoffrey Gorer argued that death had become so unmentionable in society as to be turned into the role of pornography: "There seems to have been an unremarked shift in prudery; whereas copulation has become more and more 'mentionable,' particularly in the Anglo-Saxon societies, death has become more and more 'unmentionable' as a natural process."[5] In working to deny death, to remove natural death from old age and natural causes from everyday exposure, Gorer writes, society has become more and more fascinated by *violent* and *unnatural* death: "While natural death became more and more smothered in prudery, violent death has played an ever-growing part in the fantasies offered to mass audiences—detective stories, thrillers, Westerns, war stories, spy stories, science fiction, and eventually horror comics."[6] Death becomes a fantasized, taboo topic that is envisioned in increasingly fantastical ways, removing it from the realm of the everyday. It has created what Littlewood calls something of a voyeurism of death, a consumption of it almost as entertainment.

This has never been more obvious than in our current time of mass shootings, which happen with such regularity that the incidents now must contain extra aspects of intensity or unusual natures to break through to national news. In 2012, the massacre at Sandy Hook, in which around two dozen first and second graders were murdered by a man wielding a high-powered long gun, the nation was wracked with grief because it was the first time children that young had been targeted victims.

But the shootings continued apace, and each one was memory-holed almost as quickly as it happened. That is, until 2018, when students at Majorie Stoneman Douglas High School in Parkland, Florida, experienced their own mass shooting. What shifted here was that many of the students—teenagers close to graduating—had cell phones and were able to post videos and pictures of what was happening in real time as it happened. This was the first time we had real, genuine insight into the trauma that is a mass shooting.

But rather than aiding us in coming to terms with the reality of that death, the images and gore from the mass shootings seemed to take on that voyeuristic effect, and this was never more true than in the results of a shooting in Richmond, Texas, at an outdoor mall in May 2023. A video quickly went around social media that a person at the scene had filmed. The film, lasting only a few seconds and shaky in its footage, showed blood on the ground and a pile of bloodied bodies. Visible toward the top of that pile was a small child, clearly dead.

Self-righteous white people retweeted and posted the footage, accompanied with messages that *everyone needs to see this, we need to look at this reality and confront it.* The footage became a totem of righteousness, a symbolic display of the inaction of our government in limiting guns and handwaving away the uniquely American problem of mass shootings. But in actuality, it was a voyeuristic consumption of death. It was an image of death designed to stoke fear, not a way to honor the bodies and lives of those tragically killed. The bodies were still in the process of dying, having been violently, fatally injured only moments before, and here we were, ascribing meaning to images of them without even knowing their names, stories, or lives. We depersonalized the deaths and thus became pornographers of death.

After our mother died, my brother changed careers from being a pastor with a church to a chaplain with a hospital. He works closely with the elderly and those in hospice care whose bodies are nearing their end. This has fundamentally shifted how he discusses important things in life—his children don't shy away from talk of death. For me, raised in a world where death was whispered about and discussed in euphemism, the ways in which my nieces will talk readily about people dying and funerals and plans for burial is a bit jarring. My oldest niece once told me of her plans to be turned into compost for trees when she dies, in the same manner one would talk about a future wedding or plans for a career. It's jarring precisely because we live in a culture where fear of death is taught and yet, it is seen as a natural fear to have—instinctual even.

But plenty of cultures approach death as if greeting an old friend, viewing it as a natural part of life, a thing every person must confront and understand—because that is the reality of our physical, bodily existence. Such approaches don't avoid the fear but deal with it in ways that place it in perspective. Jewish tradition is one of those. In the handbook for medical professionals about death and dying rituals that I mentioned earlier, Ellen Levine walks us through one view of death that Jewish people in the United States tend toward expressing. Levine writes, "G-d created death. Death is not meant as a punishment, but something that is natural. The knowledge that life is not forever, and that life is only given to us by G-d for a finite time, assists us in living a life full of meaning." Death, then, is a major part of what makes life meaningful—because we only exist for a short period, in physical time and space, what we *do* with that time before death is much more important than any afterlife that comes, though some Jews do believe in a form of bodily resurrection.

One thing that Jewish rituals emphasize, as Levine notes, is "the reality of death." The customs deployed are designed to honor both the dying and deceased, and those grieving their passing. Levine notes that there are two guiding principles that are relevant here: that humans are created in the image of G-d and therefore must not be altered, and, because we are created in the image of G-d, our bodies are sacred and must be cared for as well. In practice, this means ensuring that those who are close to death do not die alone—you do not leave their bedside unless you are physically ill, and once they have died, you do not leave the body alone. A "shomer"—usually a family member or friend, but in some circumstances, a person hired by family who could not be there—sits with the body at all times, keeping watch with the body so that the person is never alone until they are placed in their final resting place by their loved ones.

This practice of sitting shiva is one that, when I first heard of it as a twenty-something, grossed me out a bit. The thought of sitting for days with a dead body felt alien to my Protestant-molded mind, where death was sterile and bodies were whisked away to be hidden behind metal doors in the basement of a funeral home. Why would anyone want to spend time sitting around with a dead body? Surely it's creepy.

But I've realized, as I've learned to accept my own body and my selfhood, that shiva is a way of honoring the person by honoring the body. In modern American Protestant theology, the moment of death is instant, recorded at a precise time on a certificate signed by a doctor. At the moment of death, the body is merely an object to be dealt with, a thing that once held a beloved human. We recoil from it as I recoiled from touching my cold mother in her casket. We view the body as mere refuse left over from a life now being lived elsewhere, a soul in some heavenly plane.

Such thinking divides us from the reality that the person we know, their smile, laugh, physical gestures, and warm hugs, has ceased to be in any meaningful form. And by being so eager to hide the body, to cloak it with fear and shame and, yes, denial, we do a disservice to the reality of the dead. I am saddened to look back at my own recoil at the touch of my mother's body because I did not believe her to be a person, even in death. It is a depersonalization that makes it very hard to grieve.

So I've spent the last decade working to confront that fear in myself, that dualism that led me to reject my own mother in the moments after her death. I have worked with and learned from Jewish scholars whose tradition many Americans claim without knowing it all (if I hear "Judeo-Christian values" one more time I swear to G-d). The continued honoring of the body as the person we knew them to be, even after death, strikes me as a way to connect back with the reality of death in a way that is healthier than whatever we do now. And surely a return to understanding the body as it is, a physical being constrained by time and space and subject to the laws of physics, is better than this cultural obsession with the horror of death as a means of coping with our own mortality.

A case that sticks in my mind as it lasted much of my teenage years is that of Terri Schiavo. In 1990, Terri collapsed in her home from a cardiac arrest likely caused by low potassium levels in her blood from drinking too much fluid. As part of an ongoing battle with her weight, Terri had been on a liquid diet and was consuming ten to fifteen glasses of iced tea a day with a restricted food intake. Terri had an eating disorder for much of her young life, which is known to cause cardiac issues in young adults. She was only twenty-six.

But what might have been a simple story of a tragic death far too young, this story morphed into something far more complicated after attempts to revive Terri were only partially successful. She ended up in a persistent vegetative state, where no brain activity was detectable but she could be kept alive as long as she had proper nutrition and care. She was intubated to breathe and had a feeding tube placed to give her nutrients. Numerous attempts were made over the next few years to improve her condition, but by 1998, her husband, Michael, who had become a nurse in order to provide 24/7 care for his wife, asked that her feeding tube be removed and she be allowed to die.

Her parents, the Schindlers, who were devout Roman Catholics, disagreed, and what followed was a seven-year court battle over whether or not Terri would have wanted to die if in such a state. Her parents insisted that Terri would have wanted to be kept alive in this state, that she would not want to die here. Her husband insisted that she had made statements that she would not want to be kept alive in such a state before this incident. The court repeatedly sided with Michael in all but the very first case. In a drastic moment that brought the case to the national stage, the Schindlers lobbied the Florida state legislature to pass an emergency law that allowed then governor Jeb Bush to intervene in the case and order that Schiavo's feeding tube be put back in. In the end, Congress and then president George W. Bush (Governor Jeb Bush's brother) looked for ways to intervene but ultimately could not overcome the judge's ruling that Terri would not recover and that she would not want to live in this state. Terri was finally allowed to die in March 2005, just over 15 years from her original cardiac arrest.

Her parents insisted that Terri would have objected to what amounted to euthanasia. And maybe she would have. Once a person enters a persistent vegetative state, the access we have to their mind is gone—we cannot know precisely what their wishes would be unless they had been previously articulated. But the body still remains in a state termed "artificial life." And it is this story, and learning the full extent of it, that convinced me that a person is still a person, even in death. Death does not destroy the person. Thus, the wishes of that person still matter, even when they are no longer able to articulate them. The body still exists as a person, even if their ability to express themself has been taken away.

This is why I'm insistent, any time this topic or a similar one comes up, that people need to have advance directives, living wills, and should talk openly about death. Because it is still you, it is still your *self*, even if you are unable to articulate your thoughts and wishes in that moment. Your body matters, even in death. And if we talked about it more, dispelled the fear, and prepared for the inevitable, perhaps we would be able to comport ourselves around the fact that we have a body in healthier ways. As Gorer said nearly seventy years ago: "If we dislike the modern pornography of death, then we must give back to death—natural death—its parade and publicity, re-admit grief and mourning. If we make death unmentionable in polite society—'not before the children'—we almost ensure the continuation of the 'horror comic.'

No censorship has ever been really effective."[7] My hope is that we can eventually discuss our plans for the end of our lives at the dinner table just as we would our plans for our families, our marriages, and our careers. All of it pertains to the reality of our existence, and just as it is important to communicate our desires in living, it is important to communicate our desires in death. Even when our bodies have ceased to function, they are still who we are.

9 | THE INTEGRATED BODYMIND

Every Friday morning at 9 a.m., an alarm goes off on my phone simply reading "T." There's a box in my hall closet with supplies. I set them carefully out on my bed, hike up my boxers, and give myself a subcutaneous shot of testosterone. I started taking a low dose of testosterone in January of 2023 as part of my medical transition to achieve a more androgynous look. I've watched my body hair get thicker and heard my voice crack as I failed to hit the soprano notes in songs that once were fairly easy to sing along to. Introducing this amount of testosterone to my body was changing and adapting it in both pleasant and unpleasant ways. And I felt more connected, more at home in who I am, partly because I was the one administering the medication to myself. For someone who used to tense up and have to take deep breaths any time I got a shot or an IV placed, having to pinch my own skin and insert a needle was a frightening process that soon became commonplace. I was more familiar with my body, more aware of my own skin, and I amazed myself at how easy it was.

I'm also a little angry that it took me this long to get here. I was so scared of myself, so scared of what it would mean to be fully present in my own body, to fully integrate myself into this person that I am, that I didn't find who I am until I was nearing forty. For someone with my genetics, it's likely I won't last much past seventy, so over half my life may have been spent in fear. And that, quite frankly, sucks. For me, the disconnect from my body robbed me of the ability to truly know myself, because I was convinced for ages that getting to know myself was the *wrong* thing, that my body didn't matter, that how I moved through the world didn't change things.

There's a queer musician I've really grown to love over the course of writing this book. Ezra Furman was born and raised in Chicago and started working as a musician at twenty years old. Nearly two decades later, she has come out as trans and has a solo career where she writes songs reflecting on her trans identity and her Jewishness, as she is working on rabbinical studies now too. In 2015, she released a song that has since become something of an anthem for me. Phrased in the passive voice, eliding the prospect of a creator but not eliminating it altogether, Furman repeats the line "My body was made" at the beginning of each stanza, each one eliciting a different fact of the body. In the end, having tried to explain it away and thrown off the social beliefs, Furman writes: "My body was made with this attribute too / The need to become something totally new / Mysterious forces that don't involve you / Body was made." She owns both that her body was made and/or created but also that she is, through social transition, engaged in the practice of making herself, changing her body through both this will to change and the medical devices available to her.

The freedom ringing through those words is what I want to set down in this book, and to leave with you, the reader. But if you learn nothing else from this work, I want you to learn these basic principles: Your body is you, it is yours, it will change, and it will die. And all of that is okay. We have no need for fear, because we are who we are, integrated and whole. Our bodyminds are made to be ours. And that means getting up off the sidelines, recognizing ourselves for what we are, and taking steps to dismantle the systems that keep this fear at the forefront of all politics and culture.

YOUR BODY IS YOURS (AND NO ONE ELSE'S)

Existing as trans and queer means that a lot of people want to make comments about my body. Simply saying who I am can elicit commentary on whether or not I should do something one way or another. At its worst, I get commentary about how I have "mutilated" my body, even though I feel more whole and more myself than ever before. And what's more is that we exist in a political sphere where fear of the trans body has led to so many states legislating against the use of medicine on our bodies. For a transgender kid in my home state of South Dakota, puberty blockers are now banned as part of their gender-affirming treatment. But a cis kid who hits puberty too early? Still fine. It is the body in which they are being used that is the problem, not the medication itself. Ostensibly this is protecting children from dangerous medical intervention, but medications don't differentiate between trans and cis, and what's safe for a cis kid doesn't suddenly become "dangerous" when the kid is trans.

These kids are growing up in a universe where their body is the subject of public discourse, and discussions about their genitals, their most private bits of themselves, are considered free game for the bigot afraid of what their body may become. That has to be a weird experience—to have grown adults debating about your body, your life, your future.

And that's why this first principle is so important: your body belongs to you. Only you know what it's like to live as you. Only you experience the world through this flesh and body. Only you know exactly what's going on. There is no *you* without it, which means you get to be the authority on what happens *to you*. And that means anything and everything, from what you put in your body, to where you travel, to what you want to do in the future, is yours. At the end of the day, you're the one who has to go to sleep in this form, and that means no one else can make decisions for you, even though plenty of people will try.

I come at this from a particularly trans perspective, but one of the principles I've relied on immensely over the years is that even if someone denies me access to my health care, I'm still who I am. Even if my testosterone gets taken from me, even if I get denied access to the tools I need to make myself appear the way I want, I'm still a nonbinary queer person. That closet door broke open a long time ago, and another person's fear of my body means nothing for *who I am*. Their prejudice and fear can threaten my safety, can possibly put me in danger, which is nothing to sneeze at, but when all is said and done, they cannot make me stop being me.

And that principle is *why* bigotry becomes so violent so often that fear turns to hate violence. It is the result of a culture that has not adequately understood its own sense of fear, instead allowing that fear to drive an approach to the entirety of life. And it is a small, sad way to live.

So we take what steps we need to protect our bodies, to keep what exists from being erased from existence, and we continue on, living big, bold, and beautiful lives because, at the heart of everything, there is no other life without it. Life encased in fear is no life at all. Your body is yours.

YOUR BODY IS YOU (AND THAT'S GOOD)

I had a best friend in high school who came from a very different background than me. She had a single mother, and they lived in a trailer park. Her family kept guinea pigs and rabbits, and she introduced me to anime and Japanese cartoons. After graduation, she went to a big state school in another state while I stayed in our hometown to pursue a Bible college degree. It was the early days of social media— Facebook was a couple of years from becoming big, but Myspace, LiveJournal, and Xanga kept us in touch. And when she came back to town for a break, we got together and she commented, "You're finally filling out!" as I'd always been the skinny one of our friend group, the one who could squeeze into that size 2 dress at the store or fit my hand into a small gap in a cupboard to retrieve a fallen pen.

My eighteen-year-old self had trouble comprehending this comment on my body. I felt like I should feel weird and I did, for a bit. But to me, it wasn't the fact that I was gaining weight but that my body was noticed in any way, shape, or form. I was so deeply disconnected from my body that the fact that my friend noticed it felt strange. I didn't know what to do with the information that I still existed in physical space. I'd gotten so deep into my evangelicalism at that time that I'd unconsciously been operating as though my body didn't exist at all. I might as well have been a brain in a jar. So my friend's comment brought me back to reality in a way I wasn't prepared for, knocking me back into existence in a small but powerful way.

It took me a decade and change to realize what was going on in those moments. My body existed whether I wanted it to or not, and no amount of personal disconnect would change that. Who I am is my body and my body is who I am. I am a person who lives in Minneapolis, who drinks coffee in the mornings, who has two cats who fall asleep on my lap when I'm going to sleep. I need a CPAP machine to sleep at night. And all of that combines to make me who I am, existing in the here and now, in a body subject to physics and weather and feelings. And it is who you are, too, with your own unique quirks and tics and whatever else makes you yourself.

And that's a good thing. We are all subject to the same physical forces. We exist in the same physical space. We are all just people, trying to figure out this crazy thing called life. And that knowledge can give us a little grace and erase some of the fear that comes up. We have a duty of care to each other because we are at once different and the same and all that is good.

And this recognition also means that being moderate on issues that stem from systemic racism, ableism, transphobia, and homophobia is no longer okay. If you recognize yourself as a body subject to time, space, and living in this world, then you are beholden to recognize the same of others, to have empathy for their positions, and to recognize that their differing experiences in their own bodies are *valuable*. Dismantling a system built on fear means not only developing a sense of love and empathy but also being willing to put our own bodyminds on the line for the bodyminds of others.

YOUR BODY WILL CHANGE (AND THAT'S OKAY)

I remember when I hit puberty, I was deeply confused by what was happening. I found a small lump on my chest one night and anxiously called my parents in, worried that I had some kind of strange growth or my body was trying to kill me. My mom and dad looked at it and said, "honey, you're growing breasts." Thirty years later, my terror makes sense, as I hated having boobs. But the bigger thing for me was that I was changing—I didn't consent to that. I didn't want hormones flooding my body! I didn't want to have to start wearing training bras.

I think dysphoria is a lot more common than statistics would say. For one thing, we don't characterize simply not liking a thing about one's body as dysphoria, even if it is causing distress. Medically, the only thing that requires a dysphoria diagnosis is transgender care. But plenty of cisgender people go through life distressed by how their bodies have changed and how they feel like they are "wrong" for how their breasts look or how their stomach hangs or their nose slopes. And often this dysphoria is the result of a major change in the body—a pregnancy, a shift in ability to exercise or a change in diet, or a medical diagnosis that radically shifts how a body operates in the world.

Dealing with that change can be extremely hard. We have certain expectations of our bodies, from living in them our whole lives. And when they shift and change, it can cause a further disconnect in which it feels like this flesh is suddenly warring against us. That's how I felt when my anxiety started becoming so strong that it caused physical symptoms—I could no longer trust my body to behave in the ways I wanted it to. The anxiety caused by that created a vicious feedback loop that I was finally able to interrupt with medication in my late twenties. And now, nearly forty, I'm much more comfortable and aware of how my body has changed and able to take those moves in stride. Some of the changes I've implemented myself. Some just happened with age. Others were genetic things that popped up in my adulthood.

We have tricked ourselves into thinking we're in stasis when, in reality, we're constantly in flux. We're literally existing on a large rock that is spinning in empty space around a giant burning star. We exist in linear time, that moves forward at the same pace, day in and day out. We are subject to the laws of physics, which includes the law of entropy. We will change, and the sooner we get settled with that fact, the better. This fear of the change is at the heart of so many phobias—and it keeps people from taking the steps they need to take now.

When it came time to remove my breasts, I did have some doubts. I worried about what it would be like if I didn't like my body after, if I missed having breasts, if, a few years down the line, I wanted to go back, to detransition. And I realized, too, that if that happened, I would simply have to cross that bridge when I came to it. This was a change I wanted and could control, and I would make it happen. And if I came to regret that change or curse it, that too was a thing I was capable of walking myself through.

And you are too. Come what may, you can get through. Change, in the end, can be a good thing. It's inevitable, anyway, so you might as well go through with a good attitude.

YOUR BODY WILL DIE (AND THAT'S OKAY)

I'm at the age where many of my friends are either turning forty or already past it. My twentieth high school reunion will happen the same year this book is released. And I'm a completely different person from the one who collected that diploma two decades ago. I have, for one, more aches and pains than I thought possible. I used to be able to tie my shoe by balancing on one leg and coming to a mid-air sitting position. Now I have to grab ahold of a pant leg to force my leg to bend the proper way if I want to sit cross-legged. If I end up on the floor, it's going to take a couple minutes to get up.

For my thirty-fifth birthday, I decided I wanted to try ice skating again. I hadn't done it since college, but how hard could it be? Turns out: hard. I bought a pair of ice skates and wobbled out onto the ice, immediately falling on my butt. Two of my friends had joined me for the skate, and at one point, I was down on my knees and unable to move. One of them skated over with a hockey stick and told me to use it as a counterbalance, and eventually I got upright again. I enjoyed myself, but I knew I no longer was capable of the easy athleticism of my youth. I'm older now, and because I am subject to the laws of physics and exist within time and space, I exist in a body that is aging and, yes, dying.

And you are too. You might already have a body that has made you well aware of its mortality. A big part of growing old and growing up (not always the same thing) is recognizing that you have a limited amount of time here on earth as the person you are. We all hope that it will be nice and long, but it's also simple reality that tells us that won't be the case.

I had an online friend who became an in-real-life friend about a decade ago. He was from the Chicago area, and I was living in Chicago for a time. We went to see Radiohead together at Tinley Park, and I got to hang out with him and his wife. After I moved out of the Chicago area, they started having children and welcomed a little boy and then a little girl into their family. We chatted every so often, talking about nerd stuff. We tried to meet up the one time I was swinging back through the Chicago area after I moved to Minneapolis, but my anxiety got the best of me and I rushed home to Minnesota instead.

In 2019, he got pancreatitis. And it snowballed, collecting infections and viruses like Pokémon. At some point he had a CDIFF infection that turned right back into pancreatitis. In the middle of all of this, a pandemic started and his young kids weren't allowed to be with him in the hospital. And in July of 2020, he went in for surgery to attempt to clear out the infection and never came back out of it. He was only thirty-five.

My friend could not have predicted he would leave us so soon, but despite all efforts to cure what was wrong, he did. Death will arrive, maybe when we least expect it, or maybe we will be lucky enough to have time to prepare. But we will die—which is why it is so important that we understand that the bodies we have in the here and now are fallible and fragile and constrained within time and space. That's why it is so deeply important that we embrace what we have now, because we may never have it again.

And making peace with that does not mean nothing matters— indeed, it means that our existence here matters much more. If we only get these embodied moments, then it is vital that we do what good we can in them and ensure that our fellow humans are able to live the lives they want to live as well.

Giving up on fear is a lifelong project. As someone with an anxiety disorder, I know that all too well—it has taken me years to work through reconciling myself with my own body, with the disordered fear I felt trapped in, and with the gendered roles I found stifling. Some parts I rejected outright, like the gender, but others I learned to make peace with—as I grew to accept that my body was not my enemy, the parts of me that experienced anxiety calmed down and became manageable. It takes work, and it takes saying to myself, "this is part of who I am, but it is not the whole." The whole of me is this bodymind, this physical, animated object confined to time and space, and experiencing the present moment—the feel of these pages in your hand, the experience of reading these words. That is the moment and that is you, me, all of us. We are bodyminds, together, whole and working toward liberation.

Liberation for all means accepting that regardless of our theology, regardless of belief, we exist in the world constrained by time and space, subject to entropy, and subject to the time we live in now. This means understanding humanity as messy and terrible and beautiful and holy all at once. It is not that all bodies are beautiful and perfect but rather that all bodies simply *are*.

CONCLUSION

In 1908, archaeologists digging in a field in Austria came across a small statue that dated back to the Paleolithic era. The statue, tinted red by ochre and formed out of limestone, stands just over four inches tall. It is recognizable as the body of a fat woman, her arms resting on the top of her breasts, and her belly protruding out over stumpy legs. It's unclear if the statue was made with feet that then broke off or deliberately formed without them. The head is faceless, turned downward toward the body, and the top of the head is intricate dimpling that resembles braids plaited close to the head in a circle ending at the crown.

"A fertility idol," the men digging in that field near Willendorf declared. It and other statues like it were displayed in museums over the years, with little description cards declaring them to be Venus statues, after the Roman goddess of love and sex (Aphrodite, in the Greek myth). They assumed this origin and history because of the statue's supposedly exaggerated sexual features—she has large boobs, and the vulva are visible between the legs. This "fertility idol" mythos remained until the 1990s when anthropologists took another look.

Scholars Catherine McCoid and LeRoy McDermott proposed an alternative theory—that the statue was not an idol or figurine for fertility at all but instead a self-portrait of a real woman. The statue resembles what a fat woman would see looking down upon her own body and using her hands to feel out what her anatomy looks like for the parts she cannot see. The "exaggerated" sexual features are instead just fat. A fat lady, sitting by the fire, with some limestone and ochre for dye, made a statue of herself.

There's ongoing disagreement about this alternative theory—there does appear to be some tradition of fertility statues existing—but the Venus of Willendorf, as this particular statue came to be called, may not be one. The idea that it's just a fat woman doing a self-portrait, and not any symbol of some further belief or ideal, is one that rocked anthropology.

We can't fully know the provenance of the Venus of Willendorf, but the disagreement over the statue's meaning and origins says a lot to me as a person existing in a fat body who used to have breasts and would frequently rest my hands on them in the position seen in the statue. The desire to give that little 4.4-inch figurine some greater meaning, some larger import in the culture that existed on land in the middle of what would become Europe, 25 thousand years ago, is understandable. Surely something built that survives for tens of thousands of years *must* be important. But like the cooking vessels and broken pots uncovered in Pompeii, it could also simply be a token from the life of a real person with a real body who saw herself as worth preserving in stone. It is fundamentally ordinary, a moment of time capturing a body's soft rolls and round, sagging breasts, and an intricate hairstyle designed to keep it out of one's face while working during the day. An entirely normal body, whittling away at a tiny version of herself, and then dropping it somewhere in that land, only to be dug up by greedy hands 25 thousand years later.

The ordinariness of something once thought mystical is, at the end of the day, what our bodies are. We have no need to be afraid of our own or of others, because we are all ourselves unable to see our bodies from the outside, like the woman carving her own shape by looking downward upon her own form. Across the millennia, we and that woman are fundamentally the same, trying to make sense out of a thing we can only view through our embodied selves, tied to a specific time and place.

I find people typically have one of two responses to realizing that existence is confined to these bodies that are fallible and mutable and so very human. They either run from the fact, latching on to a dualistic idea that there must be something beyond the physical. As I've shown here, such views tend to create a sense of fear of what it means to live in the flesh, to honor the reality of our bodies, and to be people existing in community with each other.

The other reaction I've found is to be relentlessly positive, to insist that we must express a wonder and happiness about our bodies. This kind of embodiment culture is outside the scope of this project but worth mentioning here. This, too, is a kind of running from reality—it refuses to recognize that bodies can be sources of pain and upset and that change sometimes is the best course of action. Both reactions stagnate in insisting that we must have a reaction at all, while disallowing a simple embrace of reality. We live. We exist. We are our bodies, whatever that might mean, confined to time and space and subject to the laws of physics.

Why waste that precious time being afraid of our own bodies and trying to ascribe all this meaning to something so ordinary? Bodies are. Maybe they're glorious and wild wonderlands, but the more I live in mine, the more inclined I am to think that they just *are*. We exist in these bodyminds, and that is enough.

*   *   *

ACKNOWLEDGMENTS

This book wouldn't have happened without the guidance and encouragement of my longtime agent Hannah Bowman and my lovely editor, Lisa Kloskin. Thanks for pushing me to write the book that scared me.

Dani, for lending me books about Judaism and answering my silly questions in Torah study by actually taking them seriously.

Brian, for understanding my panic and helping me take breaks during the writing process.

Aubrey and Michael, whose discussion about "wellness culture" started me on the research rabbit hole that turned into this book.

Marc and Carrie, for continuing to believe in me.

NOTES

INTRODUCTION

1 *Identity: A Trans Coming Out Story*, PhilosophyTube, Accessed December 8, 2022, https://youtu.be/AITRzvm0Xtg.
2 Audre Lorde, "Learning from the 60s" (Address, Harvard University, February 1982).

CHAPTER 1

1 Hannah Peckham, "'You Don't Have a Soul': C. S. Lewis Never Said It," *Mere Orthodoxy* (blog), Accessed December 7, 2022, https://mereorthodoxy.com/you-dont-have-a-soul-cs-lewis-never-said-it/.
2 Anthea Butler, *White Evangelical Racism: The Politics of Morality in America* (Chapel Hill, NC: Ferris and Ferris: UNC Press, 2021), 58.
3 "So in Christ Jesus you are all children of God through faith, for all of you who were baptized into Christ have clothed yourselves with Christ. There is neither Jew nor Gentile, neither slave nor free, nor is there male and female, for you are all one in Christ Jesus. If you belong to Christ, then you are Abraham's seed, and heirs according to the promise." Galatians 3:26–29, NIV
4 Matthew Lee Anderson, *Earthen Vessels* (Minneapolis: Bethany House, 2011), 41.
5 Anderson, *Earthen Vessels*, 63.
6 Anderson, *Earthen Vessels*, 144.
7 Peter Brown, "Person and Group in Judaism and Early Christianity," in *A History of Private Life: From Pagan Rome to Byzantium*, ed. Paul Vayne, 1:253–67 (Cambridge: Belknap, 1987), 260.

8 Peter Brown, "Person and Group in Judaism and Early Christianity," in *A History of Private Life: From Pagan Rome to Byzantium*, ed. Paul Vayne, 1:253–67 (Cambridge: Belknap, 1987), 261.

9 Brown, "Person and Group in Judaism," 263.

10 Brown, "Person and Group in Judaism," 267.

11 Omri Elisha, "Faith Beyond Belief: Evangelical Protestant Conceptions of Faith and the Resonance of Anti-Humanism," *Social Analysis: The International Journal of Anthropology* 52, no. 1 (Spring 2008): 58.

12 Elisha, "Faith Beyond Belief": 62–63.

13 Daniel Boyarin, *Carnal Israel: Reading Sex in Talmudic Culture* (Berkeley: University of California Press, 1993), 33.

14 Joe Rigney, "The Enticing Sin of Empathy," *Desiring God* (blog), May 31, 2019, https://www.desiringgod.org/articles/the-enticing-sin-of-empathy.

15 Anthea Butler, *White Evangelical Racism: The Politics of Morality in America* (Chapel Hill, NC: Ferris and Ferris: UNC Press, 2021), 60.

16 Ray Comfort, "Ugly Baby Blindness Syndrome," *Living Waters* (blog), June 8, 2021, https://livingwaters.com/ugly-baby-blindness-syndrome/.

17 "One of the first horrible things to reveal itself in a child is the back arch. This often happens when the parent uses the word 'no' and stops the child from touching something he wanted to touch. The mom or dad then picks up the precious bundle, and instead of finding cuddly cuteness, they find the back arch of protest." Ray Comfort, "Ugly Baby Blindness Syndrome," *Living Waters* (blog), June 8, 2021, https://livingwaters.com/ugly-baby-blindness-syndrome/.

CHAPTER 2

1 J. A. Blumenthal, "The Reasonable Woman Standard: A Meta-Analytic Review of Gender Differences in Perceptions of Sexual Harassment," *Law and Human Behavior* 22, no. 1 (1998): 33–57.

2 Blumenthal, "The Reasonable Woman Standard," 33–57.

3 John M. Harlow, "Recovery from the Passage of an Iron Bar through the Head," *Publications of the Massachusetts Medical Society* 2, no. 3 (1868): 329–347. Reprinted by David Clapp & Son

4 Harlow, "Recovery from the Passage."

5 Sami Schalk, *Bodyminds Reimagined* (Durham, NC: Duke University Press, 2018), 5–6.

CHAPTER 3

1 Abel Romero-Corral, MD, MSc; Sean M. Caples, DO; Francisco Lopez-Jimenez, MD, MSc; and Virend K. Somers, MD, PhD, FCCP, "Interactions Between Obesity and Obstructive Sleep Apnea," *Chest* 137, no. 3 (March 2010): 711–719, DOI: 10.1378/chest.09-0360.

2 William James Hoverd and Chris G. Sibley, "Immoral Bodies: The Implicit Association Between Moral Discourse and the Body," *Journal For the Scientific Study of Religion* 46, no. 3 (September 2007): 402.

3 Katharina Vester, "Regime Change: Gender, Class, and the Invention of Dieting in Post-Bellum America," *Journal of Social History* 44, no. 1 (Fall 2010): 39–70.

4 R. Marie Griffith, "Don't Eat That: The Erotics of Abstinence in American Christianity," *Gastronomica* 1, no. 4 (Fall 2001): 36.

5 R. Marie Griffith, *Born Again Bodies* (Berkeley: University of California Press, 2004), 74.

6 Griffith, *Born Again Bodies*, 82.

7 Griffith, *Born Again Bodies*, 108.

8 R. Marie Griffith, "Don't Eat That: The Erotics of Abstinence in American Christianity," *Gastronomica* 1, no. 4 (Fall 2001): 36.

9 Griffith, "Don't Eat That," 40.

10 Hubbard, Scott. "Food Rules: How God Reshapes Our Appetites." *Desiring God*. November 28, 2021, https://www.desiringgod.org/articles/food-rules.

11 John Piper, "My Body: Friend or Foe?" Desiring God, May 7, 2018, https://www.desiringgod.org/interviews/my-body-friend-or-foe.

12 Aubrey Gordon, *"You Just Need to Lose Weight" and 19 Other Myths About Fat People* (Boston: Beacon Press, 2023), 23–24.

13 Lindy West, "Fat Suit Fart Attack #1: The Whale," Butt News, March 6, 2023, https://buttnews.substack.com/p/fat-suit-fart-attack-the-whale.

14 Lizzo, TikTok video, May 2023, https://www.tiktok.com/@lizzo/video/7233425426108976427?lang=en.

CHAPTER 4

1 Susan M. Schweik and Robert A. Wilson, "Ugly Laws," *The Eugenics Archive* (blog), n.d., https://eugenicsarchive.ca/discover/encyclopedia/54d39e27f8a0ea4706000009.

2 Schweik and Wilson, "Ugly Laws," n.d., https://eugenicsarchive.ca/discover/encyclopedia/54d39e27f8a0ea4706000009.

3 *Buck v. Bell, 274 US 200* (1927), Argued April 22, 1927, Decided May 2, 1927.

4 *Buck v. Bell.*

5 Michael Billinger, "Degeneracy," *Eugenics Archive* (blog), n.d., https://eugenicsarchive.ca/discover/encyclopedia/535eeb0d7095aa0000000218.

6 Brandon Tensley, "The Dark Subtext of Trump's 'Good Genes' Compliment," *CNN* (blog), September 22, 2020, https://www.cnn.com/2020/09/22/politics/donald-trump-genes-historical-context-eugenics/index.html.

7 Tensley, "The Dark Subtext," 2020.

8 Jared Mulvihill, "Cognitive Disability and Eternal Destiny," Desiring God, April 4, 2020, https://www.desiringgod.org/articles/cognitive-disability-and-eternal-destiny.

9 John Knight, "Will My Son Go to Heaven?" Desiring God, April 19, 2022, https://www.desiringgod.org/articles/will-my-son-go-to-heaven#modal-495-gjswlqi4.

10 Mulvihill, "Cognitive Disability."

11 Colin Hambrook, transcriber, The National Disability Arts Collective and Archive, "Fundamental Principles of Disability," February 2018, https://the-ndaca.org/resources/audio-described-gallery/fundamental-principles-of-disability/.

12 Nancy L. Eiesland, *The Disabled God: Toward a Liberatory Theology of Disability* (Nashville: Abingdon Press, 1994), 70.

13 Eiesland, *The Disabled God*, 91–92.

14 Sins Invalid, "10 Principles of Disability Justice," September 17, 2015, https://www.sinsinvalid.org/blog/10-principles-of-disability-justice.

15 Eiesland, *The Disabled God*, 95.

16 Eiesland, *The Disabled God*, 96.

CHAPTER 5

1 Ta-Nehisi Coates, *Between the World and Me* (New York: Spiegel and Grau, 2015), 10.

2 Rick Perlstein, "Exclusive: Lee Atwater's Infamous 1981 Interview on the Southern Strategy," *Nation*, November 13, 2012, https://www.thenation.com/article/archive/exclusive-lee-atwaters-infamous-1981-interview-southern-strategy/.

3 Note: A year later, Wright made some deeply, deeply anti-Semitic comments about Jewish people and the Obama administration, which is obviously unsupportable.

4 David A. Graham, "Jeremiah Wright Is Still Angry at Barack Obama," *Atlantic*, September 26, 2015, https://www.theatlantic.com/politics/archive/2015/09/what-ever-happened-to-jeremiah-wright/406522/.

5 Rachel Stevenson, "Sarah Palin Reveals 17-Year-Old Daughter Is Pregnant," *Guardian Online*, September 1, 2008, https://www.theguardian.com/world/2008/sep/01/palin.republicans2008.

6 Frank Wilhoit, March 21, 2018, Comment on Henry Farrell "The Travesty of Liberalism," Crooked Timber, Accessed April 18, 2023.

7 Martin Luther King Jr., "Strive Toward Freedom," in *A Testament of Hope: The Essential Writings of Martin Luther King Jr*, ed. James Melvin Washington (San Francisco: Harper and Row, 1986), 472.

8 Sharif Paget, Aya Elamroussi, and Ray Sanchez, "Jordan Neely, the man killed in chokehold on NYC subway, is remembered as an entertainer shattered by his mother's murder," May 5, 2023, https://www.cnn.com/2023/05/05/us/jordan-neely-new-york-city-subway-chokehold-death-friday/index.html.

9 Asia Takeuchi, MD; Terence L. Ahern, BA; Sean O. Henderson, MD; "Excited Delirium," *Western Journal of Emergency Medicine* 12, no. 1 (February 2011): 77–83.

10 Takeuchi, Ahern, Henderson, "Excited Delirium."

11 Physicians for Human Rights, "'Excited Delirium' and deaths in police custody," PHR.org, March 2, 2022, https://phr.org/our-work/resources/excited-delirium/.

12 Both attributed to PHR, "'Excited Delirium' and deaths in police custody."

13 Jessica Glenza, "'I Felt Like a Five-Year-Old Holding on to Hulk Hogan': Darren Wilson in His Own Words," *Guardian*, November 25, 2014, https://www.theguardian.com/us-news/2014/nov/25/darren-wilson-testimony-ferguson-michael-brown.

14 PHR, "'Excited Delirium' and deaths in police custody."

15 PHR, "'Excited Delirium' and deaths in police custody."

16 Serena Williams, "How Serena Williams Saved Her Own Life," *Elle*, April 5, 2022, https://www.elle.com/life-love/a39586444/how-serena-williams-saved-her-own-life/.

17 Williams, "How Serena Williams Saved Her Own Life."

18 Williams, "How Serena Williams Saved Her Own Life."

19 Dorothy Roberts, *Killing the Black Body*, Second Vintage Books Edition, Twentieth Anniversary Edition, 2017 (New York: Vintage Books, 1997), 9.

20 Roberts, *Killing the Black Body*, 63.

21 Roberts, *Killing the Black Body*, 80.

22 Sabrina Strings, *Fearing the Black Body* (New York: New York University Press, 2019), 202.

23 Strings, *Fearing the Black Body*, 210.

24 Strings, *Fearing the Black Body*, 210.

25 Roberts, *Killing the Black Body*, 309.

26 Curtis J. Evans, "White Evangelical Protestant Responses to the Civil Rights Movement," *Harvard Theological Review* 102, no. 2 (April 2009): 249.

27 Evans, "White Evangelical Protestant Responses," 253.

28 Billy Graham, "What Ten Years Have Taught Me," *Christian Century*, February 17, 1960, https://www.christiancentury.org/article/first-person/what-ten-years-have-taught-me.

29 *New York Times*, "Billy Graham Urges Restraint in Sit-Ins," April 18, 1963.

30 Graham, "What Ten Years Have Taught Me," *Christian Century*, February 17, 1960, https://www.christiancentury.org/article/first-person/what-ten-years-have-taught-me.

31 Russell Moore, "Crucifying Jim Crow: Conservative Christianity and the Quest for Racial Justice," *Southern Baptist Journal of Theology* 8, no. 2 (Summer 2004), https://equip.sbts.edu/publications/journals/journal-of-theology/sbjt-82-summer-2004/crucifying-jim-crow-conservative-christianity-and-the-quest-for-racial-justice-2/.

CHAPTER 6

1 Susan Stryker, "My Words to Victor Frankenstein above the Village of Chamouix," *GLQ* 1 (3) (1994): 240.

2 Gregg Johnson, "The Biological Basis for Gender Specific Behavior," in *Recovering Biblical Manhood and Womanhood*, ed. John Piper and Wayne Grudem (Wheaton, IL: Crossway, 1991), 287.

3 Matt Walsh, as quoted in *The Continually Escalating Anti-LGBT Rhetoric*. YouTube Video, 2022, https://youtu.be/RsKgJHVqlM0.

4 Kathleen Stock, *Material Girls* (London: Fleet, 2021), 92.
5 Kathleen Stock, "Lesbian Mothers Should Be on Birth Certificates," Unherd, July 21, 2023, https://unherd.com/2023/07/lesbian-mothers-should-be-on-birth-certificates/.
6 Romans 1:26–27, Berean Standard Bible.
7 Noach Dzmura, ed., *Balancing on the Mechitza* (Berkeley: North Atlantic Books, 2010).
8 Omri Elisha, "Faith Beyond Belief: Evangelical Protestant Conceptions of Faith and the Resonance of Anti-Humanism," *Social Analysis: The International Journal of Anthropology* 52, no. 1 (Spring 2008): 66.
9 Elisha, "Faith Beyond Belief," 62.
10 CMBW.org, Nashville Statement, https://cbmw.org/nashville-statement/.
11 Catharine A. MacKinnon, with Finn Mackay, Mischa Shuman, Sandra Fredman, and Ruth Chang, "Exploring Transgender Law and Politics," *Signs*, November 28, 2022, https://signsjournal.org/exploring-transgender-law-and-politics/.

CHAPTER 7

1 Gladwell, Malcolm. "Was Jack Welch the Greatest C.E.O. of His Day-or the Worst?" The New Yorker, October 31, 2022. https://www.newyorker.com/magazine/2022/11/07/was-jack-welch-the-greatest-ceo-of-his-day-or-the-worst.
2 "What we know about the coronavirus outbreak at Smithfield Foods in Sioux Falls," *Argus Leader*, April 15, 2020, https://www.argusleader.com/story/news/nation/2020/04/15/smithfield-foods-sioux-falls-sd-coronavirus-hot-spot-outbreak/5140681002/.
3 Makenize Huber, "'I lost him because of that horrible place': Smithfield worker dies from COVID-19," *Argus Leader*, April 15, 2020, https://www.argusleader.com/story/news/crime/2020/04/15/smithfield-foods-sioux-falls-sd-worker-dies-coronavirus-hot-spot/2994502001/.
4 "Rose Schniederman's April 2, 1911 Speech," Jewish Women's Archive, https://jwa.org/media/excerpt-from-rose-schneidermans-april-2-1911-speech.
5 Radio Diaries, *Planet Money*, "The Working Tapes of Studs Terkel," September 13, 2019, NPR, https://www.npr.org/transcripts/760632634.
6 Radio Diaries, *Planet Money*, "The Working Tapes."

CHAPTER 8

1 Paul C. Rosenblatt, "Grief in Small Scale Societies," *Death and Bereavement Across Cultures*, ed. Colin Murray Parkes, Pittu Laungani, and Bill Young (London and New York: Routledge, 1997), 31.
2 Rosenblatt, *Death and Bereavement Across Cultures*, 27.
3 Rosenblatt, *Death and Bereavement Across Cultures*, 27.
4 Jane Littlewood, "The Denial of Death and Rites of Passage in Contemporary Societies," in *The Sociology of Death*, ed. David Clark (Oxford: Blackwell, 1993), 72.
5 Geoffrey Gorer, "The Pornography of Death," *Encounter* 5, no. 4 (1955): 49.
6 Gorer, "The Pornography of Death."
7 Gorer, "The Pornography of Death."